First edition published in the United States of America in 2020,
and second edition published in the United States of America in 2021
by
Light Investments & Publishing LLC

Copyright © Light Investments & Publishing LLC 2021

All rights reserved

No part of this book may be reproduced, stored, or transmitted,
in any form by any method without the prior written permission of
the publisher, nor be otherwise circulated without a similar
condition being imposed on the subsequent purchaser.

All characters, companies, organizations, events and
circumstances in this book are completely fictitious, and any
resemblance to existing organizations or real persons,
living or dead, is purely coincidental.

Photos and images are stock photos posed by models, and are
being used for illustrative purposes only.
Any person depicted is a model.

ISBN 978-1-7361078-8-1
www.lipublish.com

THE LAUNDERER

Quick Word from the Author

Thanks to the hundreds of comments received from my readers, some complimenting my refreshing ingenuity and others pointing to needed corrections, I decided to publish a second edition of The Launderer. This republication was again only possible with the help of my relatives and close friends, who graciously reviewed the dozens of versions of the modified manuscript before I could republish it. Meanwhile, my father decided to completely translate the book to French (which I will soon publish) during which he took a few prose liberties that I also added to this second edition.

The characters, companies, organizations, events, and methods of laundering money described in this book are completely fictitious. I let my imagination run wild for a few months without researching the methods actually used by criminal organizations. Despite my many years of business experience, I have never closely reviewed any case of money laundering and would like to apologize to the experts of that field for the simplicity used in narrating these awful financial crimes. And actually, I hope that the elementary nature of the descriptions will allow readers to enjoy an interesting thriller and not lead to suspicious intents by using this book as a guide to questionable activities.

As some of you noted from the first edition, parts of this book almost read like a tour book of some absolutely real landmarks, restaurants and hotels where the action takes place. I have had the privilege to visit most of the places in reference, and would encourage everyone to share this experience. As you read along, I would also urge you to look at the maps and pictures of those places, which I hope will drive your enthusiasm, as much as it did mine, while I was writing the story.

This book is the first of a series called Norrid. If you enjoy reading The Launderer, stay tuned for the sequel, The Dryer, featuring Phil and Bianca's continued courage and determination while they explore the collision of business and criminal worlds.

Chapter 1

Complete and utter boredom. Nowhere to go, nothing to try.

It hasn't always been this way. It used to bring maximum excitement. The thrilling sensation of outsmarting. The taking from soulless corporations. Living on edge. Survive despite significant risks. And at the ready to board the first flight to any country that doesn't have an extradition treaty with the United States.

Phil personally visits most of these countries semi-regularly to meet a handful of sophisticated lawyers. Not the big firms kind – you know, the ones that have a useless look about them. No, Phil uses the discreet type that set up complex sets of companies and open bank accounts primed to receive numerous transfers and conveniently forget where the money comes from.

More than 20 years with Manhattan-based multinational KexCorp Industries, Phil knows everybody. A golf partner to all men with tan lines outlining their polo shirts, a running or swimming mate to the athlete wannabes, a doubles tennis partner to any single women, and a drinking buddy to associates. Phil knows how to form a valuable friendship with co-workers the minute he steps into their office. Cheaply framed family photos reveal everything. A couple of "Your wife is gorgeous" and "your kids look so happy, what a great family," and it's in the bag.

He is skilled at keeping track of otherwise useless information – the kids' ages, their chosen colleges and majors, and even anniversaries. All filed away for future pandering. His weekend house is strategically made available during school holidays. He knows exactly when to show up for a Friday night critical teenagers' football game, graduations, a significant birthday and most important: he knows to offer them high-paying summer internships.

You see, Phil is the good guy. He takes time to listen to his colleagues' depressive moments, even counseling them when they face difficult family issues. He's been known to advise brides-to-be on their flower arrangements, to loan money he knows will never be collected, and even to pay the taxi service home for his drunk colleagues.

All this co-dependent involvement in their lives earns Phil the ultimate reward: no questions asked for anything he needs. Although the individual wire transfers are numerous but small in order to fly under the radar, even he is surprised at how easily he can saunter about the office recapping last night's hockey game and get anything he wants signed-off.

He needs more than just signatures though. Phil has to avert the many hurdles of the corporation's bureaucracy to keep the schemes going. And therein lies the rub.

To stay ahead of the curve, he has accumulated detailed notes of his company's internal control weaknesses. Ironically, the most important source of this information: the company's own Internal Audit reports. This serves as the ultimate blueprint to plan his next foray into company resources. Phil always wondered why audit reports are so freely distributed, since they can be 'how-to' guides of the average fraudster.

As if this isn't enough knowledge of where the cracks are, he foolproofs by making sure to book an 18-hole golf game with the latest executive to receive the dreaded, career-ending failing marks from auditors or regulators. By the 13th hole, the golf cart is filled with empty beer cans. Phil thereby manages to obtain the details he needs to execute his next foray into company resources while disguising sobriety to near perfection.

Over the years, hundreds of thousands of wires were sent. It has been one of the most profitable and revolutionary enterprise: an undetected corporate fraud with tentacles in every department, client, and supplier.

However, after years of metastasizing his company's resources around the globe, Phil is growing stagnant and tired of the continuous plotting and exploiting of the latest company failures to his benefit. At least when this all started, it was keeping him up at night. He had been worried, stressed, yet... entertained.

Not anymore. Phil is so bored with the ease and routine of his shenanigans, that he worries about mistakes and even wonders if quietly returning the money into KexCorp's coffers could be another form of amusement.

It has become clear. Depression is setting in; he needs a new challenge. Something has to light up his intellect again, and corporate America can no longer provide that.

Worried that a sudden 'retirement' at 41 might bring suspicions about his financial independence, Phil openly talks about selling off his 1-bedroom Upper West Side apartment, his weekend Colonial Revival getaway in the Hamptons and his beloved Mercedes. So, if and when he mentions his decreasing desire to log long hours in a lower Manhattan cramped office, his colleagues will know that he is not financially restricted. It's plausible to everyone that he has enough capital to 'retire.'

Although he doesn't have any actual plan for his next steps, Phil makes his colleagues believe that he would perhaps use the proceeds of his real estate sales to open a quiet coffee shop in Bali.

"I need a new management challenge in a small and authentic business near a beach, not the cookie-cutter approach forced on managers in a multinational", Phil tells Josh, one of his long-time colleagues. Phil thinks maybe he should incorporate admiring stories of Gauguin to his rumor-filled conversations.

Today, Phil is ready. He knows that when he informs his boss, he'll need to have one hand on the doorknob, because the most popular guy in the office doesn't easily quit. Having witnessed several employees leave the company over his tenured career, he knows "the linger effect." The time between the delivery of the bad news and the taking of one's leave, is critical to be under five minutes. He knows he is going to be offered a bigger role, more money, less hours, more autonomy, a lighter workload. Or worse, allowed to go on a vacation to think before making such a consequential decision.

Yes, a vacation is exactly what he wants... an awfully long vacation.

Chapter 2

Since he had talked so much about Bali to his colleagues, Phil needs to access his mental Rolodex of feasible alternate destinations. If there was the slightest chance that anyone figured out what he had done during all these years, he needed to at least be hard to track down for a while. And of course be prepared to never come back to the United States.

Phil purchases his plane ticket on the same day that he successfully "hands in" his resignation. Buckled up in his seat, a low-profile economy seat to São Paulo, a biographical account of Gauguin's travels lying unopened on his lap. Yet, he still dreads leaving family and friends behind. Still, Phil can't believe what he was able to pull off. But the thoughts of getting caught are still at the surface. Other passengers' passports in hand look like "commission books" of FBI agents. He keeps imagining agents storming onto the plane to cuff him – not sure whether prison or embarrassment would be more painful.

If anyone discovered what he'd done, he would be nowhere to be found. There would be an air of confidence, an "evil hero" aura surrounding his memory. However, if he were jailed for a white-collar crime, that would mean total disgrace. Everyone believing he had been so foolish for thinking he could get away with such a deception.

The plane is sitting on the tarmac, lined up behind many other aircrafts awaiting departure. The Captain is not giving any updates on the flight's take-off position in the queue. Could the crew have gotten a call to stay idle while a convoy of armed cars swarm in an impressive, synchronized fashion? thinks Phil. The flight finally gets cleared for takeoff, and Phil visibly exhales as the plane reaches the "decision speed" known as V1, and a few seconds later, wheels up. The flight could still be forced to land at any east coast airport between New York and the Florida Keys. But once the monitor shows the blip of the plane is over the Caribbean Sea, Phil relaxes and falls asleep.

The economy ticket accompanied by over-cooked beef stroganoff are his last frugalities. Upon landing in São Paulo, he wants to buy a private jet. An Embraer Praetor 600 equipped with a queen size bed and a shower. Precisely. Made in Brazil, and custom built. Perfect. With his own jet, and no further qualms about flight connections to countries friendly with the U.S., he will simply follow his money. Complete freedom.

He also decides that from now on, he would reduce the number of times his passport gets copied by hotels (a common practice outside the U.S.) – he plans to literally live on his jet. Why not? It's comfortable, safe and unless he were to print his name on its side, like prominent billionaires, it's inconspicuous. Customs officers greet celebrities and executives upon landing, but procedures are minimal due to tight landing and departure windows. And countries with no extradition treaties with the U.S. are not exactly the most sophisticated. He only needs to find a competent flight crew, well-paid, and that can handle his personal necessities, such as the stereotypical lackey errand of picking up laundry. Phil is keenly aware that this lifestyle may not be the best way to meet the woman of his dreams, but maintaining discretion is more important at the moment. He allows himself to think that the perfect woman might be someone agreeable to a jet-setting life of luxury. He reflects over his custom-built final touches of his jet-home that could even host a potential amour.

Awaken by the reach of the flight attendant's attempt to serve breakfast to his neighbor, Phil stares at the dried omelette and greasy sausage before agreeing to have a tray slapped in front of him. Not too appetizing but he reasons that his palate can wait to avoid that a paralyzing hunger brings immediate translation issues upon arrival.

His eyes barely pried opened, he reaches for the coffee cup in front of him and suddenly feels movements at his feet. Although his limps are numb from hours of immobility, it is clear that someone is pulling on the briefcase that Phil had tightly squeezed between his legs since he got on. The briefcase is full of cards issued by small local banks based in many different countries. Those pieces of plastic are Phil's primary connection to his fortune. And certainly not meant to be taken by anyone.

"Hey, do you mind?" asks Phil while reaching for the shoulder of the passenger in front of him, only to realize that the seat is empty.

The pulling on his bag intensifies as it starts to slip from the grip of his feet. Phil clumsily picks up his tray, nearly showers his neighbor with coffee and juice, and stands up to step into the aisle in order to apprehend whoever is trying to grab his precious possession.

"What are you trying..." says Phil but stops short of creating a scene when he realizes that the culprit is in fact a child of about five years old who aborts his mission and jumps in his mother's arms. "Mam, would you mind ensuring that..." continues Phil while pointing his index but stops again after the mother turns her head towards the window while shaking her head, effectively educating Phil on the difficulty of keeping a child behaved for the duration of a long flight.

Phil takes a deep breath and sits back in his seat. He keeps his precious briefcase on his lap for the remainder of the flight and in a tight grip as he disembarks and gets subjected to the slow immigration process of São Paulo's Guarulhos airport.

The outside humidity hits Phil heavily when he finally reaches the doors leading to the airport's taxi line. But he feels free. The disorganized traffic and the sight of kids attempting to sell candies to drivers at busy intersections are a relief to Phil. He feels like he has disappeared from the reach of any authority potentially trying to come after him.

Hiding behind tinted windows in the back seat of the taxi, Phil releases the grip from the briefcase and passes his fingers through his hair. The sweat from his palms offers his best chance of styling his messy hair. With no accommodation booked, he is heading straight to his bank. Despite the hundreds of millions of dollars connected to the cards contained in his briefcase, actually using one of those cards to buy an airplane could prove difficult. He knows that he has to strap in for an unknown number of painful meetings with bankers and attorneys to move funds and assemble the $20 million required for the jet.

As unpleasant as the interactions and red tape deployed by the Brazilian banks are, Phil ends up meeting Gilberto Landa from Continental Bank, who he quickly befriends. Gilberto is short and skinny and less than half of Phil's body mass. Dressed casually, like the typical Brazilian, with his thick glasses and messy hair, Gilberto looks like the smart yet socially awkward college kid that makes friends by doing their homework. He can be quiet at times but surprisingly helpful as he eagerly jumps out to support Phil's every move: walking through complicated documents, translations, making copies, getting coffee, food, etc. He even sets Phil up for the weekend at his beach side apartment in Guarujá. These tactics seem oddly familiar and Phil makes a note to self of Gilberto's attentive ways.

The driver booked by Gilberto will be available at 4pm.

A weekend at the beach while waiting for his jet: not too shabby, especially that it allows for a few days incognito, away from prying hotels. And with that, Phil jumps in the car. Traffic is horrifically grid-locked, and so he takes this opportunity to fall asleep, aided by the brutal heat.

Phil thought that the simple vehicle booked by Gilberto would attract less attention than one of the many bulletproof cars roaming the streets of São Paulo. However, stopped at a traffic light, he gets awakened by a motorcyclist knocking on his window with a gun. Frozen for a moment, not understanding a word of what the man is saying – he was certainly not going to try the basic politeness of "tudo bem" learned over the past few days. Heart rate skyrockets.

While the driver is loudly arguing with the burglar-on-wheels, Phil pulls out his wallet. He knows how this works. All the guy wants is money. Sifting through the bills, he plucks out a 50 Reais note (approximately $15) and hands it through the window.

"Here you go, my friend," he says, hoping the man will understand. The mugger licks his lips, staring at the wallet. He raises the gun. "You give all," he demands.

Sweat dampens Phil's brow. "All?" He looks down at the wad of cash folded between the leather. He makes another mental note to always divvy up his bills in small, easy-to-hand-over bundles in various places on his person. This is more than any one criminal needs. However, is it really worth getting shot after pulling the biggest heist of all time? The revolver starts to shake, and Phil knows he's out of time. "Fine," says Phil as he hands him the wallet through a small opening of the taxi window. He doesn't need his U.S. credit cards, anyway, and he'll never need his New York driver's license again. But the wallet was a going-away gift from his corporate colleagues and the poignant irony of handing it over to a criminal is not lost on him.

"Telefone," the man shouts in an almost inaudible Portuguese accent, as he reaches through the window. "Give phone." Phil snatches his phone off the seat beside him and passes it through the cracked door. It was just plastic to him and the memory cards contained... no memories. He has more than enough money to replace it.

The smell of cheap gas and burned rubber waft through the window as the mugger screeches his tires and speeds away. It is actually a welcomed nasal palate cleanser to the pungent body odor that is common, sometimes accepted, in parts of the world with tropical humidity. Thank God Phil's important briefcase is still locked, safe and sound back at Continental Bank.

His heart still racing, Phil leans his head back and takes a few deep breaths. He realizes that there might be a steep price associated with life outside of a developed country. He needs to learn to be street smart or hire security guards – or both. But how much was really lost in this encounter? Phil reasons that he shouldn't magnify the dangers. Being mugged for a few dollars shouldn't be a cause for concern, especially since it's avoidable with a few mindful precautions.

No money, no cards, no phone. Oh well. Inconvenient but Phil decides to think of it as serendipitous as his car pulls up to his beach destination. At least Gilberto had paid for the ride in advance and Phil still has the only thing that he is going to wear over the next few days: a bathing suit and flip flops. He hopes that Gilberto has a gratuitous stockpile of food and a land line in his apartment, or else this could be the start of a drastically needed diet.

Finally in Guarujá, Phil pauses and smiles as he notices the sunset reflecting on the ocean. The music and animation on the beach are enchanting.

Chapter 3

It's December morning, the start of the southern hemisphere's summer. The sun is shining as Phil wakes at seven o'clock to the oscillating rhythmic sound of the waves.

When he arrived in Guarujá last night, he had really wanted to have a drink at the beach, but without his wallet, his envy quickly dissipated. This difficult realization, however, was enough to tempt him into searching Gilberto's cabinets to find a bottle of Ypioca, a Brazilian cachaça liquor fermented from sugarcane, which is abundantly harvested across the country. Unfamiliar with this spirit, a quick inhale of the bottle's neck revealed that this elixir would be a good fit. He didn't need a whole lot, after a tiring trip and an unpleasant mugging to finish the day. The little celebration only lasted an hour.

Upon awaking, the celebratory feelings are giving place to a bit of a hangover that he wants to tame with some greasy food. His usual remedy is a bacon egg sandwich that can be found at every street corner in New York. But wait... Phil continues to place his thoughts back in order and remembers that he has no money. Staying in bed won't help, he needs to activate his blood flow to get rid of the headache.

It's looking like a perfect day to walk on the beach and jump in the blue, warm water and just float for hours. Like a dozing sea lion in a thermoregulating supine position, he is able to clear his mind, and forget about corporate life so he could plan his next venture. The waves caress his feet, his mind starts rebooting, as if it were a hard drive, slowly erasing and formatting the parameters to help rejuvenate into a new life.

Around ten o'clock, Phil starts to feel that his white cheek bones are probably turning red, and his stomach is growling. The small bottle of water found in the banker's cabinet is empty and he doesn't trust the water from the tap. Food vendors on the beach are selling fresh orange juice, roasted cheese, and fried pastries. It smells amazing and there is no way that any attempted diet will last. He decides to head back to the apartment before a fasting headache sets in. Phil keeps thinking about the unbelievable irony of having a fortune in his name, yet not a penny in his pocket.

Too weak to properly search the apartment for food or even unproperly, he lays onto the bed and falls into a deep sleep. Mid-afternoon, a loud banging on the front door wakes him up.

After throwing off the covers, he gets up and opens the door, hoping this is an English-speaking acquaintance of Gilberto. And it is. Perfect American English. But the visitor is far from friendly. This tall and massive mountain of muscles barges in and Phil is violently thrust back into the room. He hits the back of his head on the kitchen cabinets, loses his balance, then falls to the side, barely holding himself on the counter with his head now in the kitchen sink.

Phil knows that he's no match from a physical standpoint and starts evaluating his options, which are few. His legs a bit jelly, holding onto the faucet with both hands, Phil wonders what kind of misunderstanding created this situation. Breathing with difficulty due to the kitchen counter pressing against his thorax, he looks around him to see if he could grab any sharp object to defend himself, but nothing is within reach. Thankfully, his assailant stops pummeling him long enough to speak.

"Where's Gilberto?"

"I don't know where he is. I'm just here by myself. Can I help you with something?" Phil asks, suffocating.

"This Gilberto guy is the most unreliable business partner," says the thug.

"What kind of business are we talking about?" Phil immediately regrets this question.

"None of your business." The thug punches Phil in the stomach. "Tell Gilberto that I was here for the delivery and he failed me again." He disappears in the time it takes Phil to momentarily erect himself from the blow.

This country is really not safe, thinks Phil. Two unnecessary aggressions in two days. "How many more before I can leave this horrific place," says Phil loudly with no visible audience.

Already weak from more than 24 hours of fasting, Phil slips out of the sink and to the floor, cramped and out of breath. This weekend at the beach is not exactly how he had imagined it, and Gilberto may not be as nice as he sounds. After a few minutes of recovery, he closes and locks the door, and crawls back into bed.

An hour later, another visitor knocks on the door. This time very gently. Phil limps to the door, his mid-section still hurting from the previous encounter. He has no intention of letting another thug into the apartment. Suddenly, he hears the faint and soft voice of Gilberto.

"Phil, sorry to interrupt," says Gilberto.

"It's good that you're here, Gilberto," says Phil, as he carefully checks the door's peephole before opening.

"You don't look well," says Gilberto, in a nurturing voice.

"Well, let's see... I was mugged last night, I haven't eaten since yesterday's lunch and your supposed business partner probably broke my ribs. Aside from that, everything is perfect," replies Phil, sounding annoyed.

"I'm so sorry, I thought I would arrive before Tiago's visit. He is a nice guy, but he doesn't like to be contradicted," explains Gilberto.

"Contradicted? Interesting way to put it. Seems like you're a glass-half-full kind of guy," says Phil sarcastically.

"I don't understand. What do you mean?" Gilberto replies with a strong Portuguese accent, noticeably wanting to avoid the rest of a tough conversation. Phil lets it go and, anyway, has no intention of getting into somebody else's dirty laundry.

Phil is now eager to move on from this beachside hideaway, acquire his jet and take-off – literally. Gilberto reminds him that business moves slowly in Latin America, and it would be a few more days before the money is transferred and perhaps another week before Phil can take possession of the jet. Phil's blood pressure is increasing at the thought of being stuck there. But first things first: food.

Gilberto takes Phil to a local eatery. Feeling infinitely better, they walk to a coffee shop to enjoy Brazilians' favorite pastime. The smell of coffee and fresh pastries make Phil forget about his ailments for a moment. They sit on stools overlooking the beach, the tireless waves, the calm ocean, slowly sipping their rich java, which makes Phil wonder how on earth could Brazilians be so blessed by such natural beauty, yet can't figure out ways to live safely.

On their way back to the apartment, Gilberto starts to fidget. "I need to get a few things. Why don't you enjoy the beach and meet me back at the apartment in a few hours?" says Gilberto.

"A few hours?" Phil suspects something is wrong. "It's already past five o'clock. What am I going to do at the beach at this time of the day?"

"Yeah, just have a few beers. Enjoy the view. Brazilian bikinis barely cover anything, you'll love what you see. Here's R$1,000. Have fun," says Gilberto with a reassuring smile.

"Thank you, but...," says Phil before getting interrupted.

"No, no, really, I insist. Enjoy the beach," says Gilberto, as he hands Phil another R$1,000 then turns and walks away.

Phil becomes seriously worried about the presumed questionable business that Gilberto is conducting. He decides to play dumb to avoid getting caught up in other criminal activities. Pretend that nothing is happening. Plus, it's much better to let Gilberto finish his dealings with his 'partner' and avoid further complications. So, Phil takes his advice and heads towards the water. He sits at a beach-side bar and orders a local Skol beer.

The humidity and the warm temperature make the beer go down smoothly. Phil relaxes, enjoys the moment, and ponders on how Brazilians seem to live so simply and easily. They appear to truly enjoy their existence. Quite a contrast from New York City, where everyone is stressed out about their work, family, commute, etc.

Brazilians are also very approachable. In just a few hours, Phil talks to more women than he has over his last five years in New York City. Gilberto's last minute extra hush money proves handy. As he watches people pack up their beach gear, he suddenly looks at his watch and thinks that it cannot possibly be that late. It's ten o'clock and hours since he last ate a sizable meal. A bit tipsy, and with a genuine smile on his face, in Portuguese he says good night to everyone sitting by the bar, and walks back to the apartment. His alcohol-weakened resolve let memories of drunken work parties creep in and for a moment, he's annoyed that no one is putting him in a free taxi.

Not a sound as he enters. Just a note from Gilberto: "I waited for you, but I had to head back to São Paulo. I will pick you up sometime on Thursday. Here's R$5,000, have fun! And oh, I installed a dead bolt on the door. Stay safe," still no phone... Maybe he can get one tomorrow at a local shop. The additional lock is only a partial stress reliever. It is also a validation by Gilberto that being in this apartment is not all that safe.

Phil undresses and gets ready for bed. Last night's oversleep, aggressions, jet lag and music from the party people on the beach through the thin walls keep him awake for a few hours. With the new curve ball of being stuck in Guarujá for a few more days, he tries to plan out the next few steps of his journey until suddenly, sleep overtakes him.

Chapter 4

Phil's rib cage is sore, and the back of his head is tender, when chirping birds wake him up at six o'clock. The alcohol from last night had provided some numbing of the pain, but that buzz is now long gone.

His first thoughts of the day drift to Gilberto's behavior; suspicious to say the least. But soon, Phil will dictate his own actions and start on a new journey aboard his jet. Just a few more days following Gilberto's mandated schedule.

First order of the day: pain killers. Then, a Brazilian breakfast would certainly be welcomed. He still has the delicious taste of local coffee encrusted in his mouth. Walking under this tropical heat is certainly worth the short distance from Gilberto's apartment.

After walking around a few blocks of this surprisingly large beach town, and not finding any shops whatsoever, Phil figures that a hotel concierge might be his best bet to obtain a phone. Certain to find a good English speaker that can provide a paper map with simple surrounding directions, he is now seeking an upscale hotel.

He comes across the beautifully manicured lawn and pristine pool of Casa Grande Hotel. This place must be willing to provide a helping hand to a lost gringo, so are called Americans in Latin America.

The lobby of the hotel reminds him of the 5-star hotels that he used to frequent as a business traveler. Some happy memories of his time as an executive rush back for a minute. But they quickly clear when Phil reminds himself of the fortune waiting for him all over the world – no more c-suite for him. Not worth it. Legally earning as much as he now has at his disposal is impossible, unless of course he had invented the little-known online bookstore called Amazon before Jeff Bezos.

The hotel staff is friendly and provides all he requests and more. Phil's gringo tips are well received and he's on his way. He finds pain killers, food, and a cell phone. Finally, life is returning to normal. As Phil is walking towards the apartment though, his mind shifts back to Tiago, the thug that served up an undeserved punishment yesterday. What if he comes back? Or worse, what if he pays him a surprise visit during the night? The dead bolt that Gilberto installed will not protect him from someone kicking in the door. His passport is in the briefcase inside the bank's vault, so checking-in to a hotel here or back in São Paulo might prove impossible.

Therefore, Phil decides to go back to the shop he found the phone to look for some kind of portable security apparatus. He finds a small wireless surveillance camera with motion detector and connects it to his new smart phone. He also grabs a fisherman's knife and a button/panic alarm. In Brazil, these items can be purchased at the same store and just as Phil likes it, no questions asked. Yep, this will do the trick for now.

Despite his worries, Phil cannot resist hitting the beach late afternoon and share drinks with the same crowd from the night before. They seem to have spent the entire day at the beach, with both men and women wearing beachwear made with scant amounts of fabric. Not quite like the strings used for women swimsuits, Brazilian swimwear for men is a tightly fitted and probably one tenth, or less, of the material used in typical American swim trunks. And the name of this male Brazilian swimwear has an almost onomatopoeic name... "sunga." Phil knows that he would never wear a sunga.

The beach-side bar crowd has started drinking early, so the clients are festive and treat Phil as their old buddy when he arrives. After making fun of his American swim trunks and the fact that he's not sure why they are called "trunks," the new friends chat him up, teaching him some Portuguese dirty words while they practice their broken English with him. Although Phil compliments them on their language skills, he can barely follow their drunken stories and just nods with a smile most of the time.

All the chatty fun stops, however, when the 9-inch television on the corner of the bar shows the start of a 'Futebol' game. The sport is divine for Brazilians, and tonight, the National Team is playing against its arch-rival: Argentina. Phil was never a fan of soccer, so after a few minutes of soaking in the admiration that his new friends have for this tiny TV, he starts gazing towards the ocean. The waves are making a mesmerizing and peaceful continuous movement and sound. His admiration of the water and the full moon gets suddenly interrupted.

"Mate, you're not from here," says a beautiful blue-eyed blonde in a white bikini walking towards Phil. He freezes for a moment, not believing her sudden appearance. If he had been standing, his knees would have certainly buckled. Phil has had a few drinks, but he knows this is not a Brazilian accent. And this bikini is made of more than just strings. No, this bikini covers yet reveals all of the fit and soft curves, thinks Phil. Also, the word 'mate' at the beginning of the sentence... Brit? Aussie? Kiwi? He is not sure. He needs to hear more words before guessing.

"Porque?" Phil tries one of the few Portuguese words that he just learned. He's confident that the word translates to "why?" or "how come" but he's actually forgotten what she said to warrant this response.

"Nice try, but you're not watching the game with the round ball. So, that's a dead giveaway that you're not Brazilian," she says, which quid pro quo, gives away to Phil that she is not a Brit. They are die-hard fans of soccer in the UK as well. She would not use the term 'round ball', which sounds more like an insult.

"Ah you noticed... I'm here, just here enjoying this beach," Phil says, visibly uncomfortable while trying to mask his New York accent. He is fumbling his words in a mix of alcohol and an attempt to hide this new-found feeling, that he is completely melting for this girl. She is beautiful and that is a term Phil realizes he's rarely ever used. Perhaps not knowing beauty until this moment? He is quite certain that he is not yet sporting beer goggles, so this must be real.

"Indeed, the natural beauty of this place is quite something, isn't it? What brings you down here? This town is off the beaten path of obnoxious New York business travelers," she says with a wide toothy grin that sends a clear message that she's just one step ahead of him.

"It's because I'm not obnoxious," replies Phil.

"Well said Mr. Manhattan. That is quiet the rejoinder," she says while nodding and trying to get the bartender's attention.

Oh, she's smart and beautiful. For a brief moment he has another realization. He is completely inexperienced with such a woman. Phil is a tall, good looking guy but with the constant "upgrading" dating experience by woman in New York, he had all but given up on meeting someone who checked all of his boxes.

"I'm Phil, it's nice to meet you. And what brings you here?" Phil says quickly with anticipation of gleaning more clues from her response.

"I'm Bianca." she says without an "r" sound at the end. So, definitely not a Brit. She is not Biancar. "I wanted to decompress in an exotic place, far from home, and away from my family until the New Year. I also needed a break from the routine and the overcrowded beaches back home. I reckon I'd travel as far as possible."

"Ah, Australia... I heard this 'reckon' business before. Crowded beaches, you must be talking about Bondi Beach in Sydney," says Phil with a playful tone, recalling a quick swim at Bondi Beach after walking the tourist packed but beautiful Bronte to Bondi trail by the water during a business trip to Australia.

"You got me," replies Bianca.

"Hey, can I get you a drink?" asks Phil, noticing that she might be trying to order from the bartender.

"Actually, I was just closing out my check. Hey, I'm meeting some friends at a house party. Join us?" Bianca casually asks. Phil is tempted but already had his fair share of surprises in this foreign land. A house full of strangers could mean trouble. But how to turn her down and still convey his interest?

"I think I got enough for tonight. I'll grab a bite here and then call it a night. Any suggestions?" asks Phil as he holds the English-only version of the menu.

Bianca had eaten there earlier and recommends not to get the half chicken black mussels pasta. Phil is completely distracted by her stunning beauty. They pause for a few seconds and look at each other in the eyes.

"Will you be here again tomorrow?" asks Phil.

"You bet, see you tomorrow," says Bianca.

She signs her check and gathers her beach belongings. As she walks out she hears him order the chicken-mussel pasta. She shakes her head causing the small metal detail ends of her hanging bikini ties to jingle. At the same moment both have a slight smile on their faces but obviously for different reasons. Phil is so mesmerized by Bianca and didn't pay close enough attention to her suggestion, and as result ordered exactly what she said to avoid.

The Brazilian mishaps suffered so far are now all worth it. Although still on his guard, Phil cannot shake off the giddiness from his encounter with Bianca. Not that he tries to. He recalls that her invitation sounded genuine with no signs of foul play.

He now definitely needs a story though. Telling her about his plans to roam the world to harvest the fruits of his corporate fraud would not exactly give him the best chance to win her heart.

Phil carefully reviews the recorded motion on his surveillance camera before leaving the bar. Some harmless back and forth in the hallway throughout the afternoon until, oh no... Tiago visited again an hour ago. He seemed to have noticed the camera and left quickly. Hopefully, that will be enough of a deterrent. Phil wishes all criminals used their minds instead of their fists, just like he did. It would make the world a much nicer place. Obviously Phil has thought about what it would be like in prison.

Chapter 5

The soreness has mostly dissipated but a dark bruise is now visible on Phil's side. Not exactly the best look for the beach, but perhaps it will distract onlookers from staring at his love handles. Phil already noticed that Brazilians are found of observing others while they relax on the beach, so he decides to avoid shirt-off situations all together.

The following three days are spent relaxing, enjoying local coffee shops and all the unique Brazilian cheese breads. And, of course, meeting his new friends at night for happy hour. After Phil finally starts showing a taste for the local drink 'caipirinha', a mix of cachaça and lime, he officially gets accepted into the circle and, as a result, becomes part of a chat group with his new drinking buddies. Although Phil is not really the texting type, agreeing to this continuous senseless messaging allows him to get Bianca's phone number, which he'd been too shy to ask for up until now.

Phil makes up a perfectly plausible business-man-on-vacation story for Bianca, and she reveals that she is a professional accountant in Australia. They exchange a warm hug on Wednesday night, promise each other to keep in touch and meet again soon. Bianca intends to stay in Guarujá for a few more weeks before the year-end work starts piling up again back home. So, Phil sees an opportunity to meet again. He'd have to find different living arrangements, though. Unless a private air strip is available nearby, living in a jet may not accommodate dates in Guarujá with Bianca.

At six o'clock in the morning on Thursday, Phil is awakened by a cell phone alert that video motion was detected at the front door. His heart is racing. He slowly turns to his side to look at his phone's screen and sees Tiago and Gilberto talking by the door. Tiago appears angry while pointing at the camera. Phil hopes that Tiago will control himself this time.

Gilberto knocks softly on the door. Phil slips a knife in his hands and looks outside before opening. No sign of Tiago. He puts the knife away and opens the door.

"Good morning. How is your vacation?" asks Gilberto with a fake smile.

"Pretty good. Why so early?" says Phil.

"I have to be in the office by 9am and we will probably hit some traffic. I'll get you a coffee while you get prepared." says Gilberto.

"Alright. See you in 20 minutes," says Phil, grumpily.

From the window of the apartment, Phil watches Gilberto walk away towards the coffee shop. Still no sight of Tiago. He then swiftly takes down the camera before hitting the shower.

While the ride back to São Paulo is thankfully crime-less, the speed at which motorcycles are passing between cars in traffic is mesmerizing. The bikers also honk continuously to keep all drivers alert and shake their heads at any car attempting to switch lanes. In summary, this is a big enough mess that Phil is happy to be nothing more than a passenger.

During the ride, Gilberto eagerly shares some good news with Phil. Enough funds were consolidated into one account at Continental bank, ready to be transferred to pay for the airplane. Gilberto has also already contacted Embraer to confirm that they have a jet available for purchase. The manufacturer just needs a few more days to retrofit the bed. Phil somewhat regrets having shared so many details with Gilberto given the mountain of suspicions about his activities with Tiago in Guarujá. If it turns out that Gilberto is a gangster, being associated with him could bring negative attention to the new pristine life, away from crime, that Phil is trying to establish for himself.

Phil is happy, however, that things are moving forward. In a week, he could be far away from all his preoccupations. Phil's immediate concerns shift to where he is going to sleep tonight. He fears another invitation from Gilberto. With access to his credit cards, safely stored in the bank's vault, perhaps he can book an AirBnB without having to show a passport.

Back in the bank's offices, Gilberto continues to act as if he were Phil's personal assistant by getting in the middle of all his plans. Phil politely asks him to back off, and starts insisting on managing things by himself, including the dealings with the Embraer sales representative. Phil is concerned that over-helpful Gilberto has some kind of angle that will lead to no good.

While Phil is on the phone negotiating the details of the jet's delivery, Gilberto suddenly shows up with his briefcase. What on earth?, thinks Phil. What is the purpose of a safe deposit box if a random bank employee can access it at will? Phil hangs up his call and starts lecturing Gilberto, who gives lame excuses about having to shift things around in the vault and having to empty his box. What was he up to? All the content seems to be in place but, Gilberto now potentially knows in which banks Phil has hidden all the money, debit card and credit card numbers. Not good.

Phil calls his Brazilian attorney, Antonio Lasia, to let him know that he is coming over to his office immediately, instead of meeting in Continental bank's offices, per previous arrangements. Phil asks Gilberto for a confirmation of the wire transfer to Embraer and leaves hurriedly. Just three blocks away from Antonio's office, Phil takes a chance and carries his luggage and valuable briefcase through the streets of São Paulo. He storms into Antonio's office, sweaty and out of breath.

"Gilberto from Continental bank is acting strangely. I think he's involved in some kind of questionable activity. He also potentially snooped through my briefcase to collect my banking information with other institutions. We need to open new accounts to safeguard all the funds," says Phil as if the building were on fire.

"You are being paranoid, but we can contact your attorneys in other countries, and send notices to your banks to ensure that funds don't move without your instructions. But this might raise some suspicions. You would be better off heading to a country without a U.S. treaty as soon as possible," says Antonio, in a mix a reassurances and cautions.

"What do you mean, isn't Brazil one of those? Why am I here, then?" asks Phil.

"I have told you years ago that extradition from Brazil is low risk but possible. It has somewhat increased lately with our new President. Since you've started to move money here, anti-money laundering regulations have become more sophisticated, and some of your account activity could raise flags," explains Antonio.

"In that case, I need to get prepared to leave this place as soon as possible," concludes Phil.

Phil borrows a laptop from Antonio and hunkers down in a conference room to deal with his priorities: a place to stay over the next few days, and a flight crew ready to depart in a week or so. It turns out that AirBnB also requires passport copies. His best chance might be with craigslist. Everything is posted in Portuguese though. After a few hours of back-and-forth between craigslist and Google Translate, he secures a small studio nearby where the landlord accepts cash. Phil also has a posting in place for two pilots with credentials to fly a Praetor 600.

Phil cannot find a good solution for the briefcase's safety. Walking around the streets with it or keeping it in a stranger's apartment both seem risky. After charging his surveillance camera and connecting it to Antonio's WiFi, Phil tests whether opening the bag creates enough motion to record. It does. He takes some of the money and cards with him and keeps them in four different pockets of his jacket and trousers. He then sets up the camera in the middle of the bag, squeezed tightly against the rest of the content. If someone opens the bag, the identity of the perpetrator will be recorded in the cloud. Finally, Phil asks Antonio to safely keep the bag in his office. As long as the WiFi connection cooperates, Phil figures this is his safest bet and the best way to test Antonio's loyalty.

Chapter 6

Phil's final days in São Paulo are filled with handling the complicated bureaucracy of the certification / registration of his aircraft, obtaining insurance coverage, and securing a landing slot at his next secret destination: Jakarta, Indonesia. Not even his new captain and first officer, Sergio and Claudio, know where they are flying to. Phil kept it vague and promised a lucrative month-long trip around the world, all paid in advance, during which the group will stay in luxurious hotels and run basic errands for him. He didn't mention that the jet will never return to Brazil. Phil intends to buy them a commercial flight if they eventually express the desire to go home. The two pilots are very excited about the opportunity to log hours on a brand-new jet and travel the world. Phil selected single guys, with few family attachments, knowing they would look at this opportunity as a once in a lifetime dream job.

Phil goes back and forth to Antonio's office during the week, with no sign of anyone opening his briefcase. That is significant for Phil. In a world of deceptive practices, even his own, perhaps he can count on Antonio and leverage that in the future. Phil sets aside his suspicions that Antonio knew this was a test. Obviously, Antonio didn't have much to gain from searching Phil's briefcase.

Over the past few days, texting back and forth with Bianca has really filled Phil's hope that he will see her again. He resisted the urge to drive to Guarujá to have a drink with her one last time before leaving. On his final day in Brazil, he finally sums up the courage to ask her out for dinner in São Paulo. She agrees immediately and Phil plans a date with her at the famous Figueira restaurant, which has a giant century-old tree in the middle of the dining room. He also prepares how he will explain his travel plans to her, the luxurious and relaxed lifestyle in romantic locations, and perhaps even send his pilots to pick her up in Australia with his private jet for a Bali vacation in the coming months. While this sounds romantic and adventurous, she may start to wonder why Phil would not visit her in Australia instead. However, a discussion about which country is on the U.S. extradition list might not bode well on a first date. Avoiding talks about Australia all together is probably better.

In the end, Phil doesn't have to find the answers to those questions because Bianca cancels the dinner plans at the last minute. She didn't find a way to safely travel back-and-forth to São Paulo, especially returning to Guarujá late at night. Phil ponders carefully whether he should invite her to stay with him tonight in his small studio. But he thinks it might appear too early and forward. It may ruin everything. Phil expresses some disappointment, but also some hope to see her again. Perhaps on the other side of the world.

As soon as Phil obtains final confirmation that the jet is ready to go, he hurriedly packs, picks up his briefcase at Antonio's office and tells his pilots to meet him at Embraer's delivery center in São José dos Campos, a two-hour drive north east of São Paulo. This time Phil takes no chances, he orders a bullet proof car service.

Following Antonio's direction, Phil portrays himself as a business executive in all his dealings with Embraer. The company would not necessarily assume that Phil was involved in a crime, but if someone decided to investigate,

Embraer employees would have to reveal any irregularities in their transactions with clients. Large criminal organizations such as drug cartels equip themselves with jets, so aircraft manufacturers can typically see which clients are legit based on certain criteria. Therefore, despite wanting to leave the country as soon as possible, Phil acts the part and carefully reviews the equipment list and all the financial details, as if the last thousand dollars mattered to him.

The pilots, already familiar with the aircraft type, review all the flight manuals, make sure the fuel is topped-off, complete their checklists and file the flight plan. They are ready to go.

A specially appointed female immigration agent comes on board at the last minute for passport inspection. Phil is clearly nervous. He knows that he doesn't have anything illegal on board nor does he have large sums of cash that could alert anyone. But his hundreds of bank cards could always raise suspicions. And the question of whether anyone back at his former employer has noticed his heist will hang over his head forever.

Sergio, the stereotypical Latino with slight dark skin and features, slick hair and with the most amazing mirrored-color-aviator glasses, is a definite smooth talker. He removes his uniform jacket to reveal his well-defined bicep muscles and starts chatting up the agent. Phil doesn't understand a word of the conversation but could swear this was happening in a beach bar with Sergio flirting and promising all kinds of things to this perfectly dressed woman.

Once the immigration agent confirms that everything checks out with limited questioning about where the flight is heading to, she deplanes with a smile – and Sergio's phone number. He turns to Phil with a smirk: "This is how you get things done in Brazil." Without actually looking at what just happened, Phil would have assumed Sergio meant bribing of officials, but it is now clear that flirtation is part of the country culture as well.

They receive departure clearance and off they go. Flying eastbound is the shortest distance, and very importantly, offers the best selection of countries that are less than friendly with the U.S. They had filed their flight plan with a refueling stop in Gabon and final destination in the Maldives. Halfway through the first leg, however, in the middle of the Atlantic Ocean, Phil alerts the pilots to change the flight plan for a fuel stop in Ivory Coast, and the final destination: Jakarta, Indonesia. After arguing with air-traffic-control for 15 minutes, the plan gets approved and the jet is re-routed. Phil had thoroughly researched the ability of doing this, but apologizes anyway to the pilots, who seem disappointed with the change. They are apparently used to shorter distances and more predictable flights. They also had dreamed of seeing the Maldives, with its breathtaking water-villa resorts.

Phil is in control again. He is routing his jet as he pleases, he has Antonio working on giving advisory to his banks all over the world, he has escaped from Gilberto and his questionable business, and more importantly, he now has a bed in his 'home'. The mattress is little stiff, and the shower is tiny with limited water supply, but Phil doesn't have to worry about where he sleeps anymore.

Phil gets comfortable and falls asleep. The rough runway of the Abidjan's airport, in the Ivory Coast, awakes him. This is the first landing of his jet. He hopes that nothing is broken. The middle of Africa would not be the best place to find spare parts. Ground control demands that the airplane stops for immigration before refueling. Two agents, armed-to-the-teeth, come onboard, close the door, and ask the pilot to keep the air conditioning on. They sit comfortably in front of Phil, who feels like this is going to be a long conversation. Phil wonders whether this is normal procedure, or if these guys just want a break to sit on his leather-bucket seats and enjoy some cold air. After 20 minutes of questions about Phil's business, for which he is making up answers on the fly, the agents query about the last-minute change of flight plan.

"Deployment of immigration agents for non-scheduled flights is expensive and requires a lot of procedures," says one agent.

"Apologies for the trouble. I understand and I am ready to pay the fees," replies Phil.

"I don't think you understand, we have lots of paperwork to fill out and the office is not opened until tomorrow. This is very inconvenient," says the agent.

It appears to Phil that the agents are looking for some sort of bribe. Unaccustomed to dealing with this type of situation, he wonders if they could be setting a trap. Phil freezes for a moment. He mentally adds up how much money he can outright spare. One of the agents starts tapping on his shotgun, as if to indicate that he is waiting for something, and to signal a position of power. With his Brazilian smooth negotiator manner, Sergio steps in.

"Can I offer you guys a drink?" says Sergio.

"That would be much appreciated," says one of the agents.

"We have aged whiskeys, Grey Goose vodka and Beefeater gin," offers Sergio.

"No need for glasses, that will do. We'll take the bottles," says the agent.

"But alcohol carry import duties, which we need to collect from you," says the other agent.

"Understood. Will $5,000 be sufficient to cover the duties?" asks Phil, starting to catch on where this conversation is leading. But he knows that his cash limit is around that amount.

"Oh! Please don't insult us," says the agent, tapping on his shotgun again.

"If you are very thirsty, we could throw in the rest of the bottles of this bar, but for more money, we would need to go inside the terminal and find an ATM," says Phil, knowing that the agents probably do not want this exchange to be publicly exposed.

"That will do. Put all of this in a suitcase that we will roll it in for 'inspection'," says the agent.

As Phil contemplates his negotiation victory, he wonders if he will have to constantly deal with such practices, given the type of countries that he plans to visit. A more immediate issue though, is being out of cash, and having to pay for jet fuel with a credit card. It will leave a trace but there is no other choice.

Phil makes arrangements for their landing in Jakarta and reserves a jet hanger for a week. And, off they depart again.

Chapter 7

Arrival in Jakarta is much smoother, the immigration service even cleared their entry over radio, no visit from custom agents. The ground crew facilitates the plane's movements to the ramp where Phil has a hanger reservation. The door is not opening though. After a 10 minutes wait, Sergio turns off the engines and opens the door. Phil disembarks and asks the ground crew to open the hanger door. It turns out the hanger is not available. A disabled jet is stuck in there. Phil's jet will have to stay on the ramp for the night.

A quick visit to the terminal allows Phil to get some local currency and snacks. He then sets up Sergio and Claudio in a nearby hotel and leaves them with bags of clothes to drop-off with the hotel's laundry service. Sergio reminds Phil to have the ground crew connect the jet to a power supply if he wants light and air conditioning throughout the night – and hot water in the morning.

Affected by jet lag, Phil spends the night thinking about ways to safeguard his assets. Perhaps buying low maintenance properties in cities with decent levels of development would be good. Real estate would surely be more difficult to steal from him, and he could always sell or rent them out later to generate cash.

Morning comes with limited shuteye. Phil would like to benefit from a few more hours of sleep but the increasing frequency of takeoffs are starting to be difficult to support. So there is, after all, a downside to living on a jet, concludes Phil after opening the window shade and offering a look of contempt towards the main runway. Coffee will have to keep him alert for the previously booked meetings with lawyers and bankers. And now Phil will add real estate agents to the list.

Jakarta is a large, densely populated city, and like many large Asian cities, suffers from heavy traffic. Parts of the city are sinking from the floods, forcing even more congestion. Therefore, Phil's commute to the downtown area is long, but uneventful. He is astonished by the swarms of scooters and how many people each one can fit. Many of them transport small infants, with no helmet or protective gear.

Phil is in command throughout the day. He doesn't let any of his advisors make decisions for him. He believes that the best way to avoid getting caught in someone's else dirty plan, is to constantly surprise them. Taking advantage of being in Indonesia, he completes the purchase of two apartments. Not enough time to properly visit them though, so sights unseen. One in Jakarta, and one in Bali, both directly purchased from the developer. Full floor penthouses, 24 hours security, with private vehicle entrances and elevators. The one in Jakarta even has a helicopter pad. Perhaps a helicopter could be helpful at some point in the future. Contracts are signed, funds are transferred, legal title directly in Phil's name is confirmed.

Before heading back to his jet, Phil asks for $200,000 in cash withdrawn from his account, in U.S. dollars, Euros and various other Asian currencies. He also sends his private banker scurrying the city with a shopping list that includes a small safe, more surveillance equipment, a laptop, three phones, a tablet, briefcases, luggage, and clothes. The banker turned personal shopper is not happy with these added duties, but he knows that his client is not kidding around.

Phil meets Sergio and Claudio back at the airport. The jet will have to stay on the ramp for another night. The hanger is still accommodating the disabled aircraft. Phil is jet lagged and exhausted, with limited energy to argue with the airport staff, despite having paid for a full week worth of hanger. As long as there is no typhoon or hail, his prized possession will be just fine sleeping under the stars, and Phil will easily close his eyes no matter what, the minute the last bit of caffeine wears off.

He installs his new laptop, ready to watch a movie, but falls asleep quickly. A few hours later, however, noise outside the plane wakes him up. He opens the curtain and watches as six men are unloading cargo from a jet parked nearby. He grabs his phone to check the time: three o'clock. The brightness of the phone illuminates his face. When he turns to look through the window again, he realizes that one of the men noticed Phil. It must have been from the light of his phone. The man points towards Phil and seems to alert his comrades. Phil ducks down. He obviously witnessed something he should not have.

Phil is pretty sure they cannot open the door from outside but grabs his knife, more out of instinct and fear than any serious intent of using it. He can hear the men talking as they approach his jet. They are now standing right outside, and Phil recognizes familiar voices. He slowly raises his body to look through the window, and in complete disbelief, notices Gilberto and Tiago amongst the men. This is too much of a coincidence, they have to be here in relation to Phil, who immediately wonders how they could have tracked him down in just two days. Their so-called 'business' has to be an organization with significant connections.

Heavy knocking on the plane fuselage, near the door. Phil wishes he knew how to fire up this jet or at a minimum, how to use the radio. Maybe he can bluff his way out. He looks again from the window. The thugs have automatic weapons, an axe and a couple of crow bars. What do they want? Phil has some cash to offer, maybe he can buy them off. He sees Gilberto overseeing the situation, maybe he is the ringleader. Phil dials up Gilberto's cell phone. He sees him pick up from his window view.

"Good to hear from you Phil," says Gilberto as he answers the phone.

"Gilberto, what are you doing here?" asks Phil.

"Oh, we were just in the area and thought we'd say 'hi' and have a drink with you."

"What do you want?" asks Phil as he raises his voice in impatience.

"We just want to come in. Open the door please," Gilberto requests in a soft voice.

"Leave now, I'm already in contact with the control tower. They are watching your every move. Cut your losses and scram before the police arrive."

"Phil, the tower is closed, and we've already cut your power supply, so the plane's radio is not working. You have five seconds to open the door," Gilberto says, now with a commanding voice.

Still watching from the window, Phil sees Tiago swing his axe right into the fuselage of the jet, near the door.

"Phil, we will tear up our own door to get into your plane, if we have to. Open the door so Tiago can calm down a little," says Gilberto.

"Tell me what you want first." Phil requests again.

"That will not be possible Phil, my apologies," Gilberto concludes and hangs up.

Phil attempts to call 911 from his mobile, but that doesn't work. There must be another emergency code to dial in Indonesia. He looks around him for any object that could be used as weapon – his knife is clearly not enough against an axe. Or maybe just something to jam the axe and grab it from Tiago. But they also have machine guns. The bullets would come right through. Phil is experimenting the literal meaning of the expression "bringing a knife to a gun fight". Tiago has already swung his axe a dozen times. The hull now has a sizeable hole. A couple more swings and they will be inside. Phil decides to adopt a diplomatic approach to reduce the anger of these men, and finally opens the door, while pleading his aggressors to regain their composure. The stairs slowly come down to the ground. Tiago races inside the plane and pushes Phil to the floor.

"Where is it?" Tiago asks loudly.

"I have no idea what you're talking about. I tried to tell Gilberto before you got all mad," replies Phil, still on the ground.

"I'm not talking to you. Gilberto, where's the money?" asks Tiago.

"Under the mattress," replies Gilberto.

Tiago yanks the queen mattress and layers of plastic sheets to a side to reveal a massive amount of cash. Instead of a proper box spring under the mattress, at least a foot thick of currency notes covers the entire surface. In a split second, Phil realizes why the bed was so uncomfortable, but more importantly, why Gilberto had gotten in the middle of ordering the jet from Embraer. He needed a mule to transport his money out of Brazil.

Phil just sits on the floor, watching these thugs collect their money. There must be close to $10 million in U.S.

dollars and Euros. The sheer amount of money makes Phil realize the magnitude and seriousness of Gilberto's criminal activities. Phil wonders how he got himself in such a mess.

Once the cash is all packed up in two vans parked just outside the plane, only Phil and Gilberto are left on the jet, looking at each other. Phil wishes he never met this monster.

"Are you happy now? How did you track me down anyway?" asks Phil.

"It's not a question of happiness. It's just survival. I don't call the shots. We tracked you down with a simple GPS device placed in the middle of the money. You should have inspected your new toy properly. You were too eager. It has come back to bite you," replies Gilberto while showing the small black box that he used to track the plane.

"Yeah, whatever, just leave me alone. And thanks for grounding my jet with all this damage."

"It's not that easy. You've seen too much tonight. I wish we could have taken the money without you even noticing or knowing that it was there in the first place. Too late now. You're coming with us. Put these on," says Gilberto as he throws a pair of handcuffs to Phil.

"Where are we going?" asks Phil.

"You'll know soon enough. Grab your passport," says Gilberto.

As they get off the plane, Phil scans the surroundings to find someone to alert. Although the control tower is closed, planes and vehicles are being moved by ground personnel a few hundred meters away. Perhaps Phil can attract their attention. So, he starts screaming and waving in their direction. No reaction from the ground personnel, who are all wearing orange noise reduction earmuffs. However, Phil gets the full attention of Tiago, who quickly grabs Phil, tapes his mouth shut with duct tape, and throws him in a van. Gilberto and other accomplices strap Phil onto a stretcher. He can't move. Gilberto installs an I.V. into Phil's arm. While he resists for a second, Phil realizes that he is now completely at their mercy.

"What are you injecting me with?" asks Phil, barely audible as his sounds get muffled by the duct tape. Phil is frightened but guesses that the injection is non-lethal. If they wanted him dead, why would they go through this trouble?

"Don't worry, you'll just sleep for a while," says Gilberto.

Phil goes in and out of consciousness for 30 minutes trying to resist, hoping to hear or see some nugget of valuable information. He sees a large ferry boat through the window, and finally gives in to sleep.

Several hours later, Phil wakes up as the van is driving off the boat. The view is definitely familiar, he is not in Indonesia anymore. Suddenly the famous skyline of Singapore becomes visible. Phil wonders how those thugs were able to get him across immigration and avoid questioning while on the ferry boat, with what must have looked like a dead body in a van. Remaining quiet while parked on the ferry certainly explains the need for him to be asleep throughout the journey. And so much for all the planning around countries with extradition treaties; Singapore is a definite friend of the U.S. Under these circumstances though, an efficient police force and a helpful U.S. embassy might be handy.

The vans drive into an indoor parking lot. Still tightly strapped on the stretcher, Phil gets rolled swiftly into an elevator, then into a cluttered apartment. Tiago finally unhooks Phil from the I.V., loosens the straps, and locks the door. Not a sound. They seem to have left Phil completely alone in the apartment. After coming back to his senses, he starts moving around his 'prison cell' room. There is lots of stuff in here, including the bags of money from his jet. Very weird.

Phil wishes to take advantage of his assailants' lapse of good sense to plan a quiet exit. He first scans the room to see if anything could be used as a weapon, in case someone were to open the door.

- Diving equipment including oxygen tanks,
- A desk and a chair,
- Office supplies: pen, pencils, tape and paper,
- Printer,
- Desk lamp,
- Curtains on a wooden pole,
- Straps from the stretcher Phil had been tied to,
- A small garbage can.

Could the pole and straps be turned into a bow? The pens and pencils wouldn't make decent arrows and the pole would probably be hard to bend. However, a few pens could be taped tightly at the end of the wooden pole to create a spear.

For an escape, using the oxygen tanks could help smash the window but sturdy metal bars block the way. If Phil could squeeze a tank between the bars and produce heat under it to generate a small explosion, perhaps the bars could bend enough to let him through. It's worth a try. Every minute that passes decreases his chances of escape.

Phil places the oxygen tank in between two bars and uses tape to secure it into place. The stretcher height is adjustable, so he positions it perfectly underneath the window, then places the garbage can on the stretcher and right under the tank. Then, he fills up the garbage can with crumbled paper balls.

It looks like Phil is on the fifth floor. Tying all the straps of the stretcher together with the curtains and the printer's power cord would create the longest possible rope, perhaps covering approximately three floors. Phil hopes that one of the bars across the window remains in place after the explosion in order to attach the rope to rappel down the wall. With more than half of the height covered by the rope, Phil figures he can either swing himself to a balcony or another object to get the rest of the way down to the ground.

Phil also prepares a protective "nest" area so that the shrapnel from the explosion of the oxygen tank don't reach him. He will hide under the desk and cover himself with the rest of the diving gear (body suits, fins, etc.) and the bags of money. He is finally ready. He yanks the cord from the desk lamp and creates sparks with the electrodes to light the paper on fire. He then goes into hiding within his nest, with his trusty hand-made spear in hand.

A few minutes pass. Smoke and smell of burned paper fill up the room. No explosion but a smoke detector goes off. Phil kicks himself for not thinking to disconnect it before lighting the fire. He takes a chance and peaks at his fire. The risk seems acceptable, so he bounces from under the desk, climbs on the chair and jumps to grab the smoke detector. As he lands back on the chair, it rolls from under his feet and Phil falls on his side. The smoke detector falls hard on the floor, breaks, and stops beeping. Phil grimaces and pulls himself back up. He is definitely hurt but cannot waste any time. He stands up, adds more paper balls into the garbage can and goes back into hiding. While he re-tucks the bags of money around himself, Phil remembers that Gilberto took his passport and money. He opens one of the bags and grabs a stack of U.S. dollars and Euros.

After another few minutes, Phil starts coughing from the heavy smoke and suddenly, his improvised explosive device blows up. The sound was louder than expected and pieces of metal fly around the room. His ears are ringing. The huge flow of oxygen in the room initially clears off some smoke but also fuels and spreads the fire to various places in the room, including near the door. Hunched from his side and back pain, Phil slowly gets up, places another oxygen tank, with the printer's ink cartridge taped on top of it, in the fire by the door. Another explosion should slow down anyone trying to come after him. If the ink cartridge can explode at the same time as the tank, it will hopefully create a black cloud in the room for at least a few seconds. Phil quickly climbs on the stretcher. The bars across the window have moved enough to let him through, just barely. As he starts rappelling down the wall, the second tank explodes, and he sees black smoke coming out the window. Success, for now.

Phil drops his spear to the ground so he can hold onto the rope with both hands. No balconies in sight but he can rest his feet on the exterior molding of the second-floor window while he is considering his next move. The explosions and smoke from the window alerted a few passers-by. They run towards the building, trying to figure out a way to help Phil. One of them runs to the street, stops a small delivery truck, and asks the driver to place his vehicle under Phil to break his fall. Great idea! Thinks Phil. He hopes that he can hold on long enough. As he is waiting for the truck to be in place, he hears the hiss of a fire extinguisher. He looks up and notices white powdery smoke coming out of the room from where he escaped. Someone is in there, putting out the fire. Phil cannot wait for the truck anymore. It is a matter of seconds before one of the thugs peeks outside and sees him hanging by the side of the building.

Suddenly, Phil senses a pull on the cord that he is hanging from. Someone is pulling on the stretcher or cutting the rope. Either way, he's in danger. Phil puts his feet back in a rappelling position, flat on the wall surface, and starts moving left and right, in diagonal, to see if he could reach a third-floor window. It's too far. But the fourth-floor window is directly under the one he came out of. As he hears Tiago yell all the words of the Bible, Phil definitely feels an upward movement. Once he gets pulled up close to the fourth-floor window, he pushes himself against the wall to create separation and momentum. As he swings back towards the building, he lands feet first in the middle of the window. His whole body goes through, breaking the glass, and he lets go of the rope. He lands in someone's living room. A thick carpet slightly eases Phil's fall. But he is bleeding profusely from the multiple glass cuts on his back, arms, and shoulders. Phil is lightheaded as he gets up.

An old lady is sitting on her recliner in front of Phil. Without hesitation, she stands up and orders that Phil sits on the sofa while she calls an ambulance. For some reason, she doesn't seem to think that Phil is a criminal, or she doesn't care. Phil notices that she uses a TTY phone for the deaf, which probably explains why she didn't seem to have heard the explosions and just calmly remained in her living room. There must have been some vibrations though. As Phil is pondering on these simple questions, his blood soaks into the sofa and he passes out.

Chapter 8

Another I.V. in his arm. This time though, Phil is in an actual hospital. He wakes up with the beeping sound of his heart rate from a machine beside him. His left hand is handcuffed to the bed. His eyes slowly open. His first sight: Gilberto and Tiago sitting across the room.

"You guys are like a bad rash. Why am I handcuffed again?" asks Phil.

"Well, you would have been less suspicious with the police if you didn't have our money in your pockets. Officers are waiting outside. Needless to say, that it's in everyone's best interest to remind you that we're all friends and peaceful tourists. While we were away from the apartment, you jumped out a window to escape a fire, which you have no idea how it got started. Simple, straight forward story, which will avoid trouble for all of us," says Gilberto.

"Give me my passport and leave me alone. You deal with your own issues," replies Phil.

"You keep confusing yourself for someone who can bark orders and make decisions. Neither of us are calling the shots here. Here's your passport, it will help your conversation with the police if they can properly identify you. But you're giving it right back to me afterwards. The quicker you come out of this predicament that you put yourself in, the better. And you're coming with us to meet the boss. He won't be happy that you burned part of his money. So, cut your losses now and stop messing around," Gilberto says as he shows a partially burned off stack of money to Phil. The fire in the room must have engulfed more than Phil had anticipated.

The friendly conversation gets interrupted by nurses coming into the room to check on Phil. The prognosis is good. The cuts on Phil's skin were not too deep, but he needed a total of twenty-nine stitches, and he has two bruised ribs. While the nurse lists his injuries, Phil gives a dirty look to Tiago, who is the root cause of his pain. One of the nurses tells Phil that he will remain under observation at the hospital for two additional days.

Soon thereafter, police officers storm into the room, and ask everyone else to leave. Phil tells them the story that Gilberto concocted. While Phil sounds quite suspicious, even to himself, no one was seriously injured and damages were limited, so the officers see no reason to charge him. They remove the handcuffs and leave.

Although not yet discharged from the hospital, Phil sits up, removes the I.V. from his arm, and examines the room to plan his escape, once again. A quick look outside reveals that he is about twenty floors up. This time, a window exit would be difficult. His clothes are in the room, so he starts dressing when suddenly he feels a burning sensation in his neck. He turns around to find out that he had yet again been sedated by his assailants. He slowly lies back down onto the bed. Gilberto and Tiago are disguised as medical professionals, ready to roll Phil out of the hospital, and into a makeshift ambulance.

When Phil wakes up, he is in an empty humid cell that looks like an old dungeon. This time, he is well secured, hands and feet plastered to a table by uncomfortable and sharp metal loops. An escape will be practically impossible now.

A tall, unknown latino-looking individual enters the tiny room escorted by heavily armed guards. He is wearing an expensive looking light-colored suit, tightly adjusted. Evidently not hostile, he probably wouldn't cause physical harm. Although he could possibly order others to do so, it is obvious that he would hate to have blood or sweat spilled on his expensive clothes.

"Phil, it's nice to finally meet you in person. My name is Ernesto," says the man with a hispanic accent.

"The pleasure is all mine, sir. It'd be better if we could shake hands, don't you think? Why don't you loosen up these ties a little?" replies Phil in a condescending tone.

"Well, I understand your feelings. But you performed above expectations down in Singapore and easily escaped us. That's actually one of the reasons why we recruited you. You have amazing imaginative talents. You will be the best asset of our team. You've also seen a bit too much of our operations to let you off the hook," explains Ernesto.

"I'm sorry Ernesto, you seem like a nice guy, but you were misled by your people. I'm not available to join your team. And you're after the wrong person. I have no criminal talents. Your efforts are wasted with me. So, if you'll just let me go now, we can all forget this has happened, and the damage on my jet will be on the account of an accident with another aircraft," says Phil, trying to act cool but is definitely worried about where this conversation is going.

"You know, the definition of crime is quite relative. I manage the finances of a large organization. My team's sole focus is to move money through perfectly legitimate companies, by-pass some bureaucratic hurdles, and generate returns for our company. These types of money movements are similar to what you have done for several years in your corporate job. The flows just happen to go in an opposite direction. You have taken perfectly legal money and made it illegal. We transform questionable money into pure bankable assets. Doesn't that make us morally better than you, actually? We strive for legality!" explains Ernesto. Phil can sense his pulse accelerate, wondering how far these criminals have spread the information about his fraudulent activities while at KexCorp.

"I see where you're going with this. What if I turn down your offer and have no interest in joining your team?" asks Phil.

"Ah Phil... This is the only team you can join. Other departments of our organization are not for you. And they're the best at tracking people, their loved ones or assets. You've had the pleasure of working with Tiago, right? He is part of our Enforcement Division. But don't worry, you will never have to fear that division again. Actually, that team will be at your disposal now, for protection and other emergencies. You also won't have to worry about production, sales and the collections parts of our organization. Let other people deal with these unpleasant activities. We'll just use your talents to move money. That's all," says Ernesto in such a calm voice, almost sounding like a preacher.

"Well, I don't have assets or loved ones, so you're out of luck with your half-baked threats. And you know what, I might not fit in any of your departments," says Phil, trying to test what Ernesto knows about him.

"Phil, don't be silly." Ernesto smiles and shows a picture of Phil and Bianca at the beach bar in Guarujá. He also shows a list of dozens of banks, which correspond to where Phil is holding his assets. "For the moment, we have frozen all of your cash until we secure your cooperation. Your jet is useless with perhaps half a million dollars of damage – and thank you, by the way, for moving our cash to Asia, we really appreciated the help. Oh, and your investment in apartments in Indonesia was a smart move, but actually using them would make you such an easy target to track down. We know the exact location of both apartments. All in all, we're really offering your best career move. I'll even throw you one more bone: you won't have to reimburse the million dollar that you burned during your half-baked escape in Singapore. You really shouldn't play with fire," says Ernesto, as if he were Phil's kindergarten teacher.

Phil is frightened by the amount of information available to these criminals. He realizes that he is in check mate, for the moment. His financial assets are probably in jeopardy and these thugs may be able to track Bianca down. Working for them might actually be his only option to save her. At least until he can figure a way out of this. Agreeing to work for Ernesto is a question of survival.

Finally out of his cell, Phil is breathing and letting his guards down for the first time in days. He is escorted by Tiago and other large men to a parking lot. Phil notices the license plates. Malaysia – that makes sense, just a short distance from Singapore. The group boards a black Chevy Suburban and drives off. Soon thereafter, Phil notices the Petronas Towers on the horizon. They're heading to Kuala Lumpur.

Phil is led to his new office in a beautiful high rise, overlooking KLCC park, in downtown Kuala Lumpur. The rich furniture, mahogany walls and bookshelves give a sense of a successful and thriving business. Phil cannot help but sport a sarcastic smile, thinking about the irony of the success of this criminal organization, and the attention to details that make it appear like a legitimate corporation.

In his first meeting with Ernesto's team, Phil is taken through the complicated organizational structure of Norrid Ltd, the top holding company, privately owned by an unnamed individual. Norrid then owns hundreds of companies globally, that all operate legitimate businesses, but also receive loads of cash to be laundered as part of their revenue. There is also significant activity amongst the controlled companies, some legitimate, some to further integrate the illegal cash by making companies look like they are buying goods and services from each other.

A particularly important Norrid human resources distinction is explained to Phil: who is 'in the know' vs. 'who is clueless'. The organization relies on various accounting departments referred to as 'Ostriches' located in every country where Norrid operates. They process all invoices in the ledgers and have no idea that anything unusual is going on. A central accounting team of 14 individuals called "Raptors", are the smartest accountant operatives of the organization. Located in Hanoi, Vietnam, and fully aware of the companies' activities, these Raptors handle special transactions and give instructions to the Ostriches while withholding any information that would reveal the nature of the money laundering operations.

Finally, a team of 20 people, located here in Kuala Lumpur, referred to as "Chameleons", handle the creation and doctoring of invoices or other documents. They are partially aware of the laundering activities and typically receive directions from each business manager, who are the only people from the legitimate businesses that are in-the-know.

The integration of cash into the various operating companies relies on proper supporting documents, which are frequently reviewed by taxing authorities, regulators, or law enforcement agencies globally. To that end, the Chameleons produce untraceable state-of-the-art documents that have never failed to satisfy questions, audits and even evidence produced in courts of law. Chameleons work closely with the Raptors on the most complex transactions or to prepare for audits by tax agencies or other government bodies. All the doctored evidence is carefully placed in meticulously organized system folders that the Ostriches can access.

The Head Chameleon is Dr. Bruno Debo, a former tax professor, with experience in all jurisdictions where Norrid integrates money back into the economy. Dr. Debo has key connections with individuals in senior Government positions, Universities, newspapers, and Law firms, who assist Norrid in various ways in exchange for free consultations with Dr. Debo on topics associated with financial markets. On a few occasions, he has even testified in front of panels full of politicians and successfully steered them away from looking below the cover of various criminal activities conducted by Norrid, its affiliate businesses, and even its competitors. Norrid's management believes that any undue attention to its industry is potentially detrimental, so helping to reduce the risk of detection of rivals' operations has been part of Dr. Debo's priorities. He also has contacts in other criminal organizations, which he sometimes leverages to avoid any of their activities causing public outrage that could have a negative impact for the whole money laundering industry.

Dr. Debo has an impeccable reputation with key stakeholders outside of Norrid, which has helped clear the suspicions that have surfaced from time to time. His involvement has reduced the need for Norrid to use methods as lethal as other organizations in order to silence people that were looking to incriminate Norrid or its staff.

Ernesto makes it quite clear to Phil that the employees in-the-know are the favorite children of the family. And you never leave your family.

"The Ostriches, Raptors and Chameleons all work under my supervision," says Ernesto with a proud smile.

"Impressive!" says Phil with a touch of sarcasm.

"As I mentioned to you before, our shareholder has other divisions: Enforcement, whom you may call upon when needed, and then Production, Sales and Collection, that you should never encounter nor ask any questions about. Makes sense?" asks Ernesto.

"I guess," answers Phil

"Good. Gilberto, whom you've already met, is a Raptor. And I would like you to be our Head Raptor, and report to me."

"What an honor!" replies Phil, with body language that communicates somewhat the opposite.

"You will soon come to love the privileges, benefits and excitement of your role, including executive living quarters right here in this building, all expenses paid and a car with chauffeur at your disposal 24/7," says Ernesto.

"This is all magnificent, but what exactly do want me to do here?" asks Phil.

"Here's your first assignment: we need you to find new ways of doing business. We seem to have exhausted the abilities of our current set of businesses. We need new ventures," concludes Ernesto and walks away. Phil raises his eyebrows, wanting to make another smart comment but it's too late. The boss has spoken.

Phil sits in his office, taking in the beautiful view of Kuala Lumpur, and wondering if an escape will ever be possible given the seemingly unlimited resources of Norrid. While nice benefits, he assumes that his office, apartment, and car are bugged and meant to keep an eye on him at all times. He had wanted a new challenge to shake his intellectual juices. But the last thing on his mind was to add to his crimes by running the reverse scenario of what he had been doing for all these years. Soon, the authorities will have a new reason to go after him.

Tiago knocks on the door, taking Phil away from his deep thoughts. Phil is still uncomfortable at the sight of this unpleasant individual. Tiago runs Phil through some security protocols and hands him a briefcase packed with his cell phone, the one he bought in Brazil, twelve fake passports, all with different names, stacks of currency for each country where Norrid operates and a gadget secured by Phil's thumbprint that generates a signal to the Enforcement Division in case of an emergency. Finally, Tiago installs a safe in Phil's office, also operated by thumb print.

As Tiago was about to leave, Phil asks about his briefcase, real passport, and bank cards. "Not available for the moment," according to Tiago.

When Phil turns on his phone, he finds pleasant messages from Bianca and alarmingly worried messages from Sergio, with pictures of the plane's body opened up. Phil sends calming messages to Sergio and asks him to arrange for the plane to be placed in the hanger that Phil had reserved, and also obtain quotations for the repairs. He also asks Sergio and Claudio to stay in Jakarta to deal with the repairs, for at least 30 days. Phil had already paid their hotel for that period anyway.

Then he turns to messaging with Bianca, who is just waking up, given the time difference. She asks him about his plans for Christmas and New Year and says she would not mind meeting him somewhere in south east Asia to celebrate, before going back home to Sydney.

Despite that his jet is grounded, Phil is completely ecstatic about the prospects of meeting Bianca again. He will need other means of transportation, though. And he won't be able to impress her by picking her up 'in style'.

Chapter 9

Innovative ideas for laundering money do not come easy to Phil during his initial days on the job. His first thoughts center around investments in traditionally cash-intensive businesses such as construction, casinos, bars, or strip clubs. But those already exist in Norrid's portfolio, so not very innovative.

Phil starts mapping out various proposals on his office's white board. Perhaps buying high value items in cash, such as cars or jewelry, and reselling them secondhand, requiring to be paid by checks or bank transfers. But the loss, especially on cars, would be too significant and it would be difficult to explain how those were purchased in the first place without revealing the purchases in cash.

What about operating a regular store, charge higher than usual margins, but offer cash rebates to customers as incentives if they are willing to pay with credit cards or checks? Phil mulls on this for a few minutes but concludes that amounts would need to be sizable to make a difference, which would in turn bring about suspicions. It would be too easy to figure out the scheme.

Phil starts browsing websites where business owners are looking for investors for their enterprises, like classifieds for business sales. Perhaps one of them would be willing to sell a business for cash. Phil realizes that a lot of import / export companies operate in the region, and from the ads, each one seems to have one angle or another. He decides to meet up with Carlos, an old man who is selling his Italian specialty food import business.

Carlos walks slowly with a visibly painful limp. His whole body seems stiff and uncomfortable. Over lunch, they talk about the type of suppliers, products and clients involved in Carlos' business. Products are imported mainly from Europe and sold throughout Asia. The man admits that his biggest challenge is currency fluctuations. Products are purchased in Euros, and by the time they arrive in Asia, their value can change significantly, from the movement in exchange rates, which sometimes makes it impossible to turn a profit. Phil becomes interested in the currency issue and asks where Carlos exchanges the various denominations collected into Euros for his purchases.

"Is it done at currency booths that we see at airports and some street corners, or in a regular bank branch?"

"Most of the time, I favor using my bank because they offer a better rate for the conversions, but sometimes I use the currency booths for convenience, small amounts or if I don't want to leave a trace," explains Carlos with a proud smile.

Not leaving a trace... That's it! Phil just found his idea. He wraps up his lunch in a hurry and thanks Carlos for his time. Back to his office, he cleans off his white board and starts designing a new scheme, which he then pitches to Ernesto.

The plan involves opening currency exchange booths in Hanoi, and bring in the cash generated by Norrid's sales from illegal operations around the world. Depending on the currency needed to be exchanged by the group on a given day, the Raptors will centrally modify the exchange rates published on the booths electronic displays to offer clients unfavorable rates. Meanwhile the attendants of the booths will be completely unaware of what is going on. Then, the Raptors will show up incognito at the booths to exchange the cash, leaving fat margins for the business. The following day, the raptors will go again to the booths to exchange the money they converted on the previous day and again be charged a fat margin. They will keep doing this until the cash has been exhausted by the many conversions, leaving margin after margin to the legitimate business. Other clients can also visit the booths to exchange funds – presumably not expecting to exchange currencies for which the rate will have been tweaked, but potentially conducting business in the other currency pairs, thereby making this operation appear even more legitimate.

Ernesto loves it. He tells Phil that he will have Norrid's Legal Team prepare all the paperwork for the business to start early January. Ernesto is so happy with Phil's idea that he tells him to take the remaining ten days of the year as a holiday.

Phil jumps off his seat and gets ready to leave the office immediately, seeing an opportunity to meet Bianca for a quick vacation. His request to get access to his bank cards gets rejected again, but Ernesto gives him $50,000 in cash to spend as he pleases during his holidays. Phil grabs his company issued briefcase, removes all the passports but the Singaporean, locks all other valuables and heads for the elevator. When he reaches the ground floor, he orders Rod, his chauffeur, to take him to Phuket, Thailand – a thirteen-hour drive.

Rod is a simple man with deep family roots in Malaysia. During the long drive, he recounts how his grandfather fought and surrendered to the Japanese during the Second World War. Rod also speaks openly about his family and is proud to tell Phil that his daughter has received a full scholarship for a medical degree in California. Phil congratulates Rod warmly but quietly wonders how such a good man could get involved with

Norrid. He hopes that his daughter will start a life in the U.S., as far away as possible from the tentacles of this awful criminal organization.

Although the cellular service is patchy at various points of the ride, Phil is able to make a reservation for a villa suite at the beach-front Sri Panwa Hotel in Phuket. Based on his limited search, this gated resort perched on a cliff should allow maximum discretion and perhaps a way to impress Bianca. Also, a suite is not too presumptuous about an expectation of a relationship with Bianca given separate bedrooms available. He sends her the details so that she can plan her trip from Brazil to Thailand.

Phil also reserves a room for the first night at the less expensive Blue Monkey Hotel near the city center, so that Rod can drop him off there and not know his location for the remainder of the holiday. Upon arrival, Phil hurries inside to check-in and tells Rod to head back to Kuala Lumpur. Rod comes in anyway to check on Phil. Good thing Phil actually had a reservation, so that he can continue his act. After some hesitation and being told by Phil that he would have to sleep in his car for ten days if he stayed in Phuket, Rod leaves. Shortly thereafter, Phil walks around town to buy a new cell phone (in case the other was bugged by Norrid's Enforcement Division), then takes a taxi to his real destination.

Checking into a luxury hotel without a credit card is unusual to say the least. Presenting a stack of $15,000 to cover the stay and the security deposit is very odd. But at this point, Phil is beyond worried about how he may appear, and with his Singaporean identity, he will probably go undetected.

As he walks around the resort to get acquainted with his environment, Phil thinks of different ways to escape from Norrid's grip. Although he truly enjoys the challenge of his new job and what he has seen of the benefits thus far, getting involved with criminals was not part of his retirement plans. He had wanted a clean start without any risk of prison time.

He gazes at the horizon, over the Andaman Sea, the peaceful water, and the silent yachts of the super-rich anchored in the bay. Phil wishes he had bought one of those before losing control of his money, it would have offered him an additional exit route. Perhaps Antonio, his lawyer from Brazil, could find a way to transfer funds despite not having a power of attorney in place. Phil decides to message Antonio in order to initiate the planning of this potential purchase. Hopefully, they can discuss that over the next few days during his holiday in Phuket, away from Norrid's surveillance.

Chapter 10

Bianca arrives the following day, beautiful as ever despite the long journey from Brazil. She is taken aback and seems uncomfortable with the luxury of Phil's villa. She is clearly not used to the finer things money can afford. Phil, as a result, also feels uncomfortable, but happy, given her reaction, that he was unable to send his private jet to pick her up!

To ensure maximum private time with Bianca on the first night, Phil orders room service for dinner, which they share on the stunning balcony overlooking the sea. Bianca recounts her last few weeks in Brazil, which had become increasingly boring, drinking with the same people every night. Phil secretly hopes that her boredom had something to do with his departure from Guarujá. She also shares that she is dreading her return home given all the work expected in the coming months, the busiest time of the year for accountants, and to face pressure from her parents to be a successful professional. Phil offers to let her know if he becomes aware of a position that she could apply for. He is of course thinking about bringing her closer to him, but not in a horrible criminal organization, that presumably traffics narcotics to generate all the cash that Phil has to help launder.

Phil and Bianca spend the following week growing closer, enjoying flirtatious moments at the beach, snorkeling in the sea, and savoring the delicious seafood served by the resort's restaurants. They also progressively become romantically involved in their villa, and eventually only need one of the bedrooms. Phil is extremely proud to walk hand-in-hand with Bianca throughout the resort; and for the first time of his life, he has found a relationship that lets him escape, just for a moment, his otherwise stressful existence. He wishes he didn't have to hide such a significant part of his life to Bianca, but given the circumstances, he doesn't see an alternative.

Thanks to her education and background, Bianca can also hold interesting conversations with Phil. He finds himself staring at her as she explains her views of geopolitical issues facing the world. She becomes especially passionate and fired up during socio-economic discussions despite Phil's teases of the boring nature of her accountant job.

Phil touches base with Antonio several times during the week. While Phil doesn't want to share all the details of his interesting interactions with Norrid's representatives, especially in front of Bianca, who is sitting next to him most of the time, he asks Antonio to check on availability and status of funds with various banks. After further research, Antonio confirms that most funds were frozen by banks after being flagged as suspicious for money laundering, except approximately $5 million that is still available in Brazil in the accounts that were used to fund the purchase of the jet. To avoid that these funds also get frozen, potentially from Norrid's influence, Phil asks Antonio to immediately arrange for the purchase of a yacht for approximately that amount. He will rely on Antonio to make a judicious purchase and have it available somewhere in Southeast Asia over the next few weeks. Also, Antonio promises to send formal notices to the banks that have frozen Phil's funds in an attempt to make them loosen up. He is not optimistic, however, that this could be done quickly without proper source of funds documentation. Norrid's agents might have created a big mess for Phil.

The night before Bianca's flight to Australia, she decides to sightsee in the town of Phuket since they have spent the whole vacation in the resort. The concierge advises the couple that Phuket restaurants are not exactly Michelin-rated institutions, and instead recommends to remain in the resort to enjoy the fine cuisine offered by the exceptional restaurants. Bianca thinks that the hotel's concierge is just biased, and given her adventurous nature, insists that Phil shows her around town. Phil remembers that the Blue Monkey Hotel seemed safe and the lobby restaurant appeared acceptable. The couple take a taxi to the Blue Monkey.

A few moments after they sit for dinner, Bianca suddenly looks very uncomfortable.

"What's wrong?" asks Phil.

"A tall creepy man in a dark suit keeps staring at me, he is freaking me out," replies Bianca, with visible fear in her eyes.

As Phil slowly turns around, he is in complete shock to see Rod sitting at a table 20 feet away. Phil admits to Bianca that he knows this man and asks her to remain seated while he heads over there.

"Rod, what are you doing here? I asked you to go back to Kuala Lumpur. You work for me, remember?" asks Phil angrily but with a low voice to avoid alerting Bianca. He also fakes a smile and shakes Rod's hand to make it look like he is reconnecting with an old buddy.

"Sir, I received orders to follow and protect you during your entire holiday. I was really concerned to have lost you sir. The hotel told me that you had already checked out. I had to call in some help, a few agents are on their way." Rod pauses as Phil lowers his head, thinking about the disaster that Norrid agents could create if Bianca were to encounter them. "Sorry sir... but I am quite happy to see that you are doing well," says Rod in an apologetic tone.

"Look, I don't need your babysitting. Go back to Kuala Lumpur and tell whoever sent you to check on me, that if they want me back to work in a few days, they better leave me alone," commands Phil.

"Sir, are you still returning to Kuala Lumpur tomorrow? Should I wait for you nearby?" asks Rod.

"Fine, but keep low profile. I don't want to see your face or any other agent until late tomorrow. And it better be the last time that you disobey my instructions," says Phil.

Rod and Phil give each other a hug to continue the impression of old friendship. When Phil sits back with Bianca, she is clearly unhappy.

"What was that about?" she asks

"Nothing, just an old buddy," replies Phil

"Why was he staring at me and why did you want me to stay at the table while you talk to him?" Bianca asks with a puzzling look.

"Listen, he has always had a reputation of being a bit of a lunatic around girls, so I didn't want to make you feel uncomfortable with him," Phil replies, but is dying inside for having to lie to her again.

"Ok but be careful in the future. This behavior was odd. It seemed like you wanted to keep information from me," concludes Bianca, as she doesn't want to create any drama during their last night together. Phil feels awful. He wishes he could just spit out all the truth.

Phil walks with Bianca around town before heading back. He wants to ensure that they are not being followed by any other agent of Norrid, so he constantly watches over his shoulder to look for suspicious people or vehicles. After thirty minutes, Phil feels confident that no one else is trailing them.

During the taxi ride back to the resort, Phil receives the jet repair quote from Sergio: a whopping $650,000. It is amazing what a dozen of axe swings can get you. Through text messages, Phil gives the safe combination to Sergio and directs him to use $175,000 as deposit with the repair vendor, and to share the remaining $25,000 with Claudio for their salary and living expenses for the next two months. He wants them to stay close to the plane in alternating shifts.

Before leaving the resort, Bianca insists that Phil promises to visit her in Sydney soon. In a weak moment of contemplating her beauty, making sure that she understands the strong feelings he has for her, and not knowing what excuse to give her, Phil agrees to travel to Australia soon, despite his self-imposed travel restrictions. In order to continue the momentum of their beach-side romance, he suggests to meet in Cairn, a northeastern Australian city near the Great Barrier of Reef.

Chapter 11

Back to work in Kuala Lumpur, Phil finalizes the setup of the new currency booth division of Norrid. Until they can figure out the exact flows of the business, Gilberto will act as manager to oversee the staff that will operate the 20 booths installed in various places in Hanoi. New employees are selected based on their ability to follow instructions, not necessarily based on their intellect or experience. Actually, Phil tells Gilberto to avoid smart people or those that would have too much knowledge about currencies and exchange rates. The staff needs to be diligent, loyal and honest but not exceedingly clever to avoid that they figure out the scheme.

The Raptors also add two additional staff members given the increased workload that the frequent visits to the booths require. Each Raptor visits one booth per day and then waits an additional three to seven days before revisiting the same booth. To avoid that any other employee or third party recognizes a pattern, the Raptors developed an algorithm to randomly determine the visits and the currencies that would be exchanged. And they only leave the unfavorable exchange rates on the screens for a few minutes. Any inquiring employee is told that markets change constantly, and the central team changes the rates to reflect what the company can exchange in global financial markets at the exact moment when the rates are posted.

After only a few months of operations, the booths are laundering serious money, which gets funneled up to Norrid's head office regularly. In fact, so much cash is generated that Norrid's treasury department notifies Ernesto that it currently lacks investment opportunities at the top of the house and wants to keep most cleaned money in Vietnam for the time being.

Ernesto sees this as a nice problem to have. He is proud of the team's accomplishments and wants to reward Phil for being such a game changer in the money laundering industry.

"How can I show my appreciation for your hard work without giving you means to escape?" Ernesto asks Phil.

"Giving me this opportunity is already the best reward you could have offered. I really enjoy working here," lies Phil.

"That is music to my ears. You know what, I'll test your loyalty. Let me pay off the repairs on your jet – as long as you promise to always let me know your flight plans in advance," proposes Ernesto.

"This would be great, and I guess that's the least you can do since you're responsible for the damages in the first place," says Phil with a provocative but mocking smile on his face.

"That's no problem, we'll get that sorted out," says Ernesto.

"And Ernesto, you'll need to either let me access my money or pay me a salary, if you want me to come up with more ideas. I need money to fuel up my jet," says Phil with the attitude of a teenager.

"Of course, we'll pay you $20,000 in cash every week, retroactive to January 1. Tiago will leave it in your safe on Fridays, that way you actually have to be here to collect it. Please spend wisely without bringing any attention to yourself," says Ernesto, in a paternal tone.

"I guess that will do for now, thank you" says Phil. He knows that this is a great salary but pales in comparison to the money in his now inaccessible bank accounts. More importantly though, Phil knows that Ernesto wants to give enough money for Phil to be comfortable but not enough to attempt an escape. Unless Phil gives up his jet, his mobility is now dependent on picking up his money at Norrid's office every week. Ernesto's grip is powerful.

Phil also shares concerns with Ernesto regarding the large amounts of laundered money sitting in bank accounts, which Norrid's Corporate Treasury cannot accommodate. If the scheme continues at the same pace, Vietnamese authorities might soon start asking questions and sniff around the business. Authorities are already aware of the "popularity" of the operations and have exchanged letters with Norrid's Legal Team – not on the volume or margins per se, but just to make sure that the company had proper internal controls to handle the cash, which forced Phil and Gilberto to use the service of guarded armored vehicles. Those vehicles themselves also bring unwanted attention from passers-by. Therefore, Phil suggests to open currency booths in other countries to spread the risk. And keep smaller amounts of cleaned money in a variety of local banks covering as many countries as possible.

Phil also recommends to Ernesto that Norrid implements a second wave of the currency conversion scheme. The additional booths would be opened world-wide and should be located near all the legitimate businesses of Norrid. Before cash is to be laundered by any of the businesses, it would be passed through the unfavorable currency conversion of the booths, thereby allowing a few percent more laundered cash every day. If implemented across all of Norrid's businesses, it should make a material difference for the group, perhaps even absorbing all the excess cash generated by its illegal activities. If not, the cash can be passed through the booths multiple times before being integrated through the legitimate businesses.

Ernesto cannot hide his excitement as he contemplates Phil's brilliance. He calls in the Legal Team to map out the implementation of this new foray.

Given Ernesto's enthusiasm, Phil takes the opportunity to let him know that as soon as his jet is back to service, he will take a few weeks off to roam around the Pacific. Without being too specific, he mentions the Fiji Islands, New Zealand, New Caledonia and the Solomon Islands – purposely avoiding to mention Australia. Ernesto is such in a good mood that he agrees immediately.

Phil works tirelessly for a month, every single day in the office, to implement the second wave. Each of the twelve target countries have different permit rules to build, install and operate currency exchange booths. Three or four of the operations in countries with more advanced economies will open in the coming weeks, while the others will take up to six months to be functional. Gilberto will have to travel all over the world to handle the hiring of staff and additional Raptors in these satellite offices, which should give breathing room to Phil, who feels that Gilberto's persistent presence is suffocating and choking his every movement.

Phil now feels that progress is good enough to justify his holiday, especially since his jet is now back to service. Sergio and Claudio land the jet in Kuala Lumpur to pick up Phil, who screens every corner of the aircraft looking for any surveillance or geo-positioning device. Everything checks out. Phil tells Sergio to file a flight plan to Auckland, New Zealand, but he warns him to be prepared for a change halfway through the flight.

Chapter 12

After three months apart, Phil and Bianca finally meet in Cairns, and promise each other to meet more regularly in the future. Phil is glad to have left Gilberto in full control of the booths' operations because he plans to fully enjoy this holiday with Bianca, filled with daily water activities, hiking adventures, dining at the finest restaurants, and of course, making up for lost time at night.

The love birds become increasingly comfortable with their intimacy. One evening, past midnight, with no one else enjoying the pool, Bianca playfully undoes the straps of her bikini top while hugging Phil in the deep end. The intimate piece of fabric slowly falls to the dark bottom of the pool as the couple kiss intensely.

"I like when you hold me tightly in your arms as if I were the only thing that mattered to you in the whole world," whispers Bianca.

"You definitely are... but it also matters that I properly cover up your exposed chest," says Phil with a smile.

"Really? Let see," says Bianca, as she releases herself from Phil's arms and swims in different directions, with Phil trying to catch up with her.

When they finally decide to continue their fitness program back in their room, Phil must dive multiple times before finally retrieving the bikini top, and Bianca, arms crossed over her chest, has a teasing smile every time he comes up empty handed. She even jokingly offers to leave it in the pool and walk back with half her attire. Phil not only refuses to share any sight of Bianca with anyone watching from their room but is worried that kids would find the delicate beachwear at the bottom of the pool in broad day light, the following morning.

Back in the room, Phil is showering when suddenly Bianca enters the bathroom and continues her spirited play, this time removing both pieces of the swimwear while dancing and pretending that a pole is anchored in front of the shower door. She then slowly opens the door to carry her act under the soft and subtle droplets from the rain-shower head above them. Phil cannot believe the sheer luck of having met Bianca as she performs a full body scrub on him. He is in paradise.

Wanting to extend the adrenaline and memories of this trip, Phil asks Bianca to take him to the Australian outback for a wild adventure. Bianca bursts out laughing, reminding him that the outback is the remote interior area of the country; some 20-hour drive. Phil still doesn't want to reveal that he has a jet parked less than five minutes from the resort, so he drops the outback experience idea. Bianca recommends the Great Barrier of Reef instead, just a short boat ride away.

While planning their activities with the hotel's concierge, Phil notices a brochure about Green Island, off the coast of Cairns. Back in the room, he investigates the island, only to find out that it houses an exclusive resort. This would be the most discrete way to spend his holiday with Bianca. There is no way that anyone at Norrid would find him there. While Bianca finds this plan too extravagant, being an accountant after all, she agrees to a two-day trip to the island.

Phil buys yet another burner phone, grabs a few stacks of cash and leaves everything else in the hotel safe before heading out on their island adventure. He wants absolutely no way for anyone to reach him. Getting in a taxi to leave the hotel, Phil notices two large SUVs arriving at the hotel. His heart stops for a moment, wondering if these men are Norrid's operatives because they look completely out of place. He relaxes as he sees four Asian men getting off. He has not seen a single Asian person on Norrid's Enforcement Division staff, so he feels confident they are unrelated.

At the Cairns pier, they sit at the lobby bar of the Marina Shangri-La, as instructed by the agent from the Green Island resort. Phil and Bianca order back-to-back tropical drinks while they wait for their boat ride, which is now 30 minutes late. Finally, a well-mannered and apologetic Vietnamese man in his sixties, with a good English, approaches and welcomes them to a speed boat docked nearby.

The humidity, wind and engine vibration combined with the fruity vodka-based drinks bring Phil to a state of relaxation, quasi sleep. When the boat slows down after the 20-minute ride, Bianca slaps Phil hard on the shoulder. Heavily armed guards are waiting for them on the dock, and the dense overgrown vegetation doesn't give the impression of an expensive resort. Once the boat is properly docked and the engines are off, Phil asks the captain if he is sure that they are at the right place. The captain turns around and commands that Phil and Bianca step onto the dock, strip down to their underwear and give all their belongings to the guards.

Phil quickly scans around him to make photographic memories of the surroundings, evaluates his options, and concludes that they need to surrender. He wonders how the Norrid operatives were able to trace them so quickly and he feels awful that Bianca needs to be part of one of these episodes. Phil's mind is set on revenge towards

Ernesto, especially after having helped him so much the last few months. How could he insult Phil like this?

Phil continues to register items that they pass as they are led to a small bungalow. A garbage container, propane tanks and a low fence, probably meant to keep animals. Let's see if an escape is possible. Propane could turn out useful. Inside the bungalow, they are tightly tied with ropes, their hands behind their back, to a low horizontal two-inch pipe running along the wall, approximately six inches from the floor. The kidnappers leave and lock the room. Phil and Bianca sit side-by-side on the floor, with their hands uncomfortably bound behind their backs.

Bianca is quiet but clearly distraught. Tears are rolling down her cheeks. Phil knows that he has gotten her into trouble but now is not the time for a long explanation. It is better to plan their exit.

Phil asks Bianca to move close to him and expose her ties to his hands to see if he can loosen her bindings. Her wrists are so tiny, perhaps she will be able to slip her hands out of the ties. For several minutes, they both try to move their shoulders and sit back-to-back to get their hands as close as possible, to no avail. Phil and Bianca realize that the pipe is so close to the wall and the floor that it is impossible to twist their bodies to get close enough together.

Phil notices that the pipe is old and rusty near the junction with the wall. Perhaps they could pull and bend the pipe enough to break it. It's worth a try. Phil asks Bianca to imitate his movements as he leans forward on his knees and squeezes his feet under his butt and then over the pipe. Their feet are now flat on the wall and their bodies are leaning forward. They are both pushing against the wall, pulling the old pipe towards the middle of the room. After a few minutes, the pipe bends slightly but clearly not enough to break off and Bianca's back is starting to hurt from the arching and pushing in an awkward position. So, they move their feet back in front of them and sit on their rear-ends again. They notice that their hands can now move more freely due to the slight bend of the pipe, and they are able to turn their shoulders and backs towards each other much easier. Phil is able to reach Bianca's ties and after several minutes, Phil can loosen the ropes enough for Bianca to free up her hands. As she starts working on Phil's ties, they hear the door unlock. Bianca sits back into place, as if her hands were still tied.

The Vietnamese man from the boat enters the room with a stern look on his face, in clear contrast to the helpful manner that he employed to lure Phil and Bianca onto the boat, pretending that he was taking them to Green Island. Although probably not very strong, the man looks slim and fit. Staring at his pointy shoes, Phil wonders whether he is a trained interrogator or torturer, and they are about to witness a scene similar to a cliché of an old James Bond or Jackie Chan movie.

"Good afternoon, my name is Li. It is a true pleasure to welcome you to this island. Not exactly the island you expected, but beautiful anyway," says the man while flashing his stained teeth with an awkward smile.

"The pleasure is really ours," says Phil with his best sarcasm.

"Sir, we have been watching your movements in Vietnam and have found your innovation unbelievably masterful," says Li.

"Thank you. It would be a pleasure to give you a tour of one of our currency booths, if you of course help us out of here," says Phil as he is slowly realizing that Li is probably not part of Norrid, unless there is some kind of power struggle within the organization.

"That won't be necessary. Instead, we would like you to sell the business to us. We have greater needs than you as far as cash management is concerned. We would of course be delighted to keep you as part of our management," explains Li.

"I know this is going to sound confusing to you but I don't own the business, and I am sure that my superiors wouldn't allow a sale, nor free me up in order to work for you," says Phil, as Bianca looks at him in distress. She knows that a proper and legitimate business sale wouldn't happen this way. Her heart rate shoots up in her confusion about what these men are talking about.

"I'll let you reflect on that until the morning. Perhaps you will realize that working for me is the only value that you have left. And finally, we are well equipped with security operatives to ensure you would remain safe if you were to agree to work for us. On the flip side, the same security personnel could keep you here, against your will, for a long time," says Li as he exits the room.

Phil cannot believe that he is now faced with a second criminal consortium with terrorist means. He gains a new appreciation for the relative safety of the U.S. and wonders if his larcenous past has irrevocably put him in the hands of dangerous people for the rest of his life.

Bianca is now in a bad mood. She is smart and has figured out that Phil is part of some questionable business. She sobs quietly as she continues to work on Phil's ties.

"You're involved with some dangerous people. How could you drag me into this?" asks Bianca, as heavier tears are rolling down her cheeks.

"I'll explain later, I promise. But first, we need to figure a way out of here," says Phil.

Once Phil's hands are freed, he comforts Bianca for a few minutes as his mind shifts to masterminding their escape.

An air conditioning unit is wedged inside a window. While it could be just pushed outside to create an opening, Phil is not sure what it would fall on, and how much noise it would create. Plus, maybe parts of the unit could be useful, so pulling it inside might be better. Phil also notices that the door of the room opens to the inside, so the hinges are accessible. Therefore, the door could be opened if Phil found some kind of tool to remove the hinges. Parts of the AC unit might be helpful for the job, so it is settled, then. He'll pull it inside the room.

Phil asks Bianca to stand near the door and let him know if she hears any noise from their kidnappers. He unplugs the AC unit. Suddenly, everything is quiet. Phil and Bianca stand still for a few seconds to see if anyone noticed that the AC has stopped. All they can hear are speed boats in the distance and buzzing insects. Phil gently removes the plexiglass from around the unit and pulls it in. It's very heavy and it almost slips from his hands. Bianca comes to help him, and they slowly ease it to the ground. The window is near the ground, so no rappelling needed this time. They move the heavy unit to block the door to slow down anyone coming after them.

Phil takes the tie ropes and the pieces of plexiglass with him. Broken into pieces, the sharp edges of the plexiglass could be used as weapons. It isn't much, but something was better than nothing. Phil goes through the window first, then helps Bianca out. They quietly circle the bungalow, crawling under the windows to avoid detection. They stop by the garbage container, from which Phil grabs pieces of cardboard that he uses, along with the ropes, to assemble a make-shift skirt for Bianca. She had been embarrassed and uncomfortable in her underwear for the last few hours.

Bianca and Phil make their way to the dock. The same speed boat that they rode in earlier is still there. They hop in. No key. Phil opens all the compartments and finds blankets, life jackets, an anchor and paddles. He knows that they can't paddle this heavy boat back to the shore, but if they can get far enough, another boat could come to their rescue. Anyone other than these criminals would be a relief at this point. Phil unhooks the boat and pushes it off the dock with a paddle.

The sun is setting. The darkness brings enough cover to quietly float away. They know generally in which direction to go as they see shore lights on the horizon. The shape of the boat, however, makes paddling very difficult. Phil and Bianca lie on their stomach on each side of the embarkation, trying to paddle as best as they can for two hours. After the sun completely sets, they pass by an island, lose sight of the shoreline and suddenly, it becomes so dark that they do not know in which direction they should be going. Complete disorientation. Bianca is distressed and makes sounds that could lead to detection as sound travels well over calm water. Phil suggests to anchor here and sleep under the blankets and life jackets. The morning sun should help to get back in the right direction. Phil cracks the plexiglass to create pointy objects. He holds one in each hand as he tries to fall asleep next to Bianca.

The temperature drops quickly in the darkness and wind starts to pick up. Their body heat is not sufficient. They both start to shiver and hold each other tightly to conserve the remainder of their warmth, but Phil worries that this won't be enough.

Chapter 13

As soon as the sun comes out, Li's crew easily spots their stolen speed boat, less than 100 meters from the island's shore. They approach slowly and see Phil and Bianca in hypothermia, drowsy and seemingly confused. Li is furious but holds back his anger – for the moment.

Phil and Bianca are brought back to shore and locked again into the same room, this time handcuffed and hanging by their hands from the ceiling. Their feet are a few inches off the floor. They come back to their senses as the hypothermia wears off. Bianca is struggling with the strain of the position, over-stretching shoulders, elbows, and wrists. Breathing also becomes very difficult as their lungs get awkwardly squeezed by the extension of their bodies. Phil painfully watches Bianca as she grimaces through the pain. He feels awful for having drawn her into this situation.

How could Phil pacify Li? He cannot possibly offer parts of Norrid's business or even help Li to compete with his own currency booths. Phil would end up stuck in the middle of two organizations, both probably ready and willing to kill a double agent. Would there be a way to broker a partnership between the two competitors? Norrid would not offer a participation in a business already in operation, but perhaps a new venture would appeal to both. As Li said, they both have cash management needs, so perhaps a vehicle to manage that cash could work.

Phil looks at Bianca again. Although she might never forgive him for drawing her into this mess, Phil really loves her and getting her back to safety is the priority. While Phil's idea is not fully developed, he decides to yell out for Li to come to negotiate a way out.

Li lets Phil undergo mental anguish for another 30 minutes before finally entering the room. Phil wants to explain his proposal to Li.

"I have an idea for you, which will help both of our organizations," says Phil.

"I'm listening," replies Li.

"Letting you invest in the existing currency booths might attract the attention of authorities, which I'm sure you are also trying to avoid. But what if I were to convince my superiors to let you launder through our currency booths. Also, our shared clean cash from the booths could be a mutual investment in a new venture, half-and-half owned by my organization and yours. What do you think?" suggests Phil, eyes wide opened, trying to make sure that Li is listening intently.

"That is a good start but what will that new venture do with all that clean cash?" asks Li.

"It will be an investment fund. A totally legit investment fund that will buy instruments in the capital markets, producing better returns than what you could ever imagine," explains Phil.

"How would it be better than other investment funds out there?" asks Li.

"Because we will employ the best investment managers, analysts and traders. They will want to come to work for us because they will earn top salaries from the fund itself, plus side benefits that we will afford with our joint cash from questionable sources. We'll pay for their housing, exotic cars, entertainment in Asia's best clubs and much more. Wall Street type of guys will love this proposal," says Phil, with the smile of an explorer that just discovered the promise land.

Li orders his guards to lower Phil and Bianca, asks that their clothes be brought back to them, and brings them to his office.

"Phil, I like your idea. But how do I make sure that you deliver on all of this?" asks Li.

"Do you really think that I want to experience this again? And we can do the company setup today. I will call my boss and we can get going right away," pleads Phil.

"What about the girl? How do I know that she won't just run to the police?" inquires Li.

"She'll work with us. She's smart and very capable. And on the other hand, if anything happens to her, and I mean anything at all, I'm out of the picture, I'd never lift a finger for you. You might as well kill me now and forget about all the money we could make together," threatens Phil while pointing at Li. "This is a great opportunity for you. You're going to get the best money laundering and investment management capabilities without even having to set it up yourself."

"Ok, we got a deal. You have two days to set it up. I'm not letting you and the girl out of my sight until everything is structured," concludes Li.

Phil maps out the scheme on paper, takes a picture and sends it to Ernesto. When they finally get in touch, Ernesto is surprised to hear from Phil, especially that he is in

Australia. Phil explains that he met someone who could be a great partner for Norrid in order to invest all the laundered money, which is anyway too material for the Norrid's corporate treasury department to handle. Phil also pretends that the partner is already an expert in managing funds but would benefit from the currency booths scheme. It would be a win-win situation with each partner contributing the same amounts of cash into the booths. Finally, creating a joint venture with an organization of similar laundering needs makes a lot of sense for Norrid, explains Phil. Ernesto says he needs 24 hours to have this approved by Norrid's seniors. As far as he knows, for the otherwise very secretive operations of the organization, it would be the first time that Norrid would invest in a joint venture. Phil reminds Ernesto that such arrangements are very common in the business world and it may even make Norrid look more legitimate. Further, it could reduce Norrid's exposure vis-à-vis government agencies if anything were to turn sour.

Phil and Bianca can finally relax in a comfortable bed, after two days of tumultuous events. Bianca whispers in Phil's ear that she is petrified by what's happened, especially that she has now heard Phil describe money laundering schemes in details. She wants to go home. Phil promises that once the business is setup, he will get her home safely. He honestly hopes that it will be the case, however, based on what he's seen of these organizations' capabilities, he knows that fulfilling this promise might take some time. But it's better to keep her calm for the time being by showing confidence about the outcome of this mess.

Ernesto calls at six o'clock to confirm Norrid's agreement to the proposed joint venture. He wants Phil back in the office to complete the deal. Phil knows that Li would never let that happen, so he convinces Ernesto to get all the paperwork completed today, before their new partner changes its mind or worse, makes a deal with another organization, and potentially competes with Norrid to create a bidding war to attract the best investment managers to run the new business.

Ernesto assembles the Legal Team, who hurriedly prepares all the material to form the new company. Each partner of the joint venture will earn units of the fund equal to its cash contribution. In practice, this means that the more each partner launders cash through the booths, the greater share of the fund's profits it will earn. The board of directors and management of the fund, however, will always be equally nominated by the partners, irrespective of the amount of cash brought in by each organization. Li's organization uses a Hong Kong based company named Goang Limited, an apparently fully legitimate corporation, to invest. The new joint venture will be called Equit, and be based in Singapore, where low taxes and a friendly business environment will attract the best employees from around the world.

Li couldn't be happier. This new venture will provide an avenue with even greater opportunities than he expected. So, he treats Phil and Bianca as royal guests for a sumptuous dinner back at the Marina Shangri-La in Cairns. Bianca is not in a festive mood, but she plays along as she is scared to death. Li announces, as everyone is ready to leave for the night, that he will take them back to the jet and put them on their way to Singapore to get Equit up and running right away. The reference to the jet earns Phil a dirty look from Bianca as she finds out, on the spot, that Phil owns an aircraft. Given the revelations of the past few days, she immediately wonders whether Phil is some kind of drug dealer to be able to afford his own airplane. Phil doesn't want to argue in any way that would make Li believe that he would not go along with the deal, so he just nods.

During a quick stop at their hotel to pick up their belongings, Phil and Bianca are flanked by Li's security detail. As soon as they enter the room, he tries to make amends by rubbing her shoulders. "Leave me alone, you've already done enough wrong," says Bianca with her head down, throwing her clothes into her luggage. Heavy tears are rolling on her cheeks. Phil doesn't insist and steps out onto the balcony, away from Li's thugs for a few seconds, to call Sergio.

"We are departing to Singapore in less than one hour, please have everything ready to go," commands Phil.

"No problem sir, everything okay?" asks Sergio.

"Everything is fine. Has anyone been near the jet, or worse, been inside?" Phil asks.

"A few Asian men approached us on the first night, claiming to want to buy the jet from you. They wanted to see the inside, but we didn't let them in. And there was no movement on the security cameras, sir. They left a business card if you want to call them," explains Sergio.

"Okay. I'll be there shortly," says Phil as he realizes how closely Li and his troops have been watching him.

Li tells his driver to park near the jet to facilitate the loading of luggage.

"No worries, we travel light," says Phil.

"Well, we have a heavy freight to send to Singapore." Li announces as his men pull three large bags.

"What is this? I'm not your mule. This is not getting on my plane," says Phil categorically.

"Phil, be reasonable. We have to show good faith to your bosses. This is our seed capital for our new venture: $11 million. If you were to show up empty handed, how will Norrid believe that we are a partner they can trust? Please run this money through your booths for us," says Li in a paternalistic voice.

"Li, we all trust you. I don't need to bring your cash on my plane. Actually, according to what we just agreed, it's your responsibility to deliver your cash to our offices," says Phil.

"Phil, I insist, and I don't like to be contradicted. Do as I say," says Li as he opens his jacket to reveal a revolver.

"This is unbelievable. You start our new partnership with a threat? Fine, we'll take your money, but stop surprising me with stuff. In the future, everything has to be planned in advance. And we're not going to start threatening each other with weapons for every aspect of managing our new business," concludes Phil. Li offers a slight smile as he buttons up his jacket.

Phil tells Li's men to leave the bags by the bed. He now knows the best hiding spot for such a large sum of cash, but remains extremely worried about his plane being searched by customs officers.

Chapter 14

Fairly certain that nobody is listening to their conversation on the jet, Phil explains to Bianca the details of his life since landing in São Paulo a few months ago – but leaves out everything about his years of corporate fraud. Bianca tells Phil she wished they had never met. Phil is hurt but fully understands. He holds her hand and promises to figure a way out of this mess.

Phil avoids showing his own emotions and concerns in front of Bianca, but he is completely frightened by what is going to happen next. He is now faced with two criminal organizations in a joint venture. While setting up Equit was a good way to save their lives when threatened by Li, the chances of anything good coming out of this new venture are remote. And Li's aggressive behavior, seemingly ready to even pull out his gun at an airport, is making Norrid's operatives look like good guys.

Upon landing in Singapore, Phil is nervous about clearing immigration and customs. The cash could get him sent to prison for a long time. Bringing more than two packs of chewing gum is considered smuggling in Singapore, so imagine $11 million.

When the immigration agents enter the jet, Phil and Bianca are lying in bed, both scared and shaking from the anxiety. They pretend that they just woke up when the plane landed. Phil fakes a few yawns, stretches his arms, and adopts an annoyed attitude, as if he were a rock star arriving in Singapore and having to go through bureaucratic procedures. Sweat is starting to form on his forehead. He is hoping that Sergio quickly pops out of the cockpit to help reduce the tension.

Bianca had removed her shirt and pulled down the straps of her bra before landing. She makes it look like she is surprised and offended that people are boarding the plane and holds the bed sheets above her chest with her arms, pretending to be nude under the covers, in an attempt to make the agents uncomfortable about asking her to move away from the mattress. Phil is impressed with Bianca's smoothness and ruse.

"Ma'am, could you please cover up?" says one of the agents.

"I am covered up... with bed sheets. Is it your intention that I step out of bed naked to grab some clothes?" asks Bianca.

"No mam, you should remain where you are. Can we please examine your passports?" asks the agent.

Phil hands over the passports. The agents scan the pages for a few minutes, and only ask a couple of questions about the purpose of their trip, then leave. What a relief! Phil has the feeling that, one of these days, his luck with immigration and custom agents will run out.

He repacks all the money in the bags and asks Sergio to be ready to leave at any time. He wants to keep his options open for a quick exit with Bianca, or maybe discreetly have her leave on her own. Whatever escape opportunity presents itself, Phil is confident that the jet will be needed, so the pilots need to be available within minutes.

Phil and Bianca get on a minivan taxi with the large bags of money loaded in the back. Per Phil's directive, Gilberto is waiting for them at the Marina Bay Sands, the famous Singapore hotel with three massive pillars topped by a boat-shaped overhang. They check into the presidential suite, from where they will operate for a few weeks as they are setting up the new business.

Phil watches closely as the bell boy loads the luggage on the cart. Coming off of the elevator, one of the bags of cash, which is made of nylon, touches a metal corner and tears open. A few stacks of money fall on the floor. Phil quickly picks them up, but the bell boy noticed. Unfortunate.

Once in the room, they lock the money into a closet and agree that one of them would always be in the room to keep an eye on the cash. Phil doesn't yet fully trust Gilberto but since Ernesto and a few Raptors are aware of the money, Gilberto would take a significant risk if he were to meddle with the cash.

Within a week, five of the Raptors have moved into the suite with Phil, Bianca, and Gilberto. They are able to clear approximately $200,000 per day, both from Norrid's and Li's operations through the 25 currency booths that were set up in the city state over the past few weeks. They now have enough clean funds in Equit's accounts to start operating, but it will take weeks, perhaps months to clear all the cash that Li left with Phil.

Next step: attract the best fund managers. Phil contacts a few recruiting agencies and explains how he is ready to pay top dollars and provide living quarters, luxurious cars, and other allowances for the best money managers in the world. The Raptors will have to scour the city to find landlords, car dealerships and other vendors willing to accept dirty cash while of course leaving no records, and absolutely keeping all the new employees in the dark about how the benefits are paid for.

Despite initially refusing to help in any way, Bianca warms up after a few days and agrees to lend a hand for certain activities that she doesn't consider criminal. Her accounting and general business skills prove very valuable to properly set up Equit's ledgers, processes and interactions with the shareholding companies, Norrid and Goang. Phil notices that she actually seems to be enjoying her participation in this operation, which warms his heart a little, especially since they hadn't had any time alone with the growing number of people crashing the suite, and her general disgust of having to get involved in crimes.

The greatest surprise comes during a pillow talk when Bianca reveals to Phil that she quit her job in Sydney and told her family that she was getting involved with a startup in Singapore. She makes it sound like it is the safest thing to do, to avoid her employer and family looking for her, or maybe worse, alerting authorities. However, given Bianca's flirtatious smile as she recounts the conversation with her boss in Sydney, Phil prefers to believe that she just could not imagine being away from him. In his mind, leaving a job that she hated doesn't even come close to the pleasure of their sudden inseparability. By the power vested in Norrid's criminal organization, Phil and Bianca are bound by the fear of attempting an escape.

Gilberto handles most of the errands for the team. As he goes down to the lobby, on his way to catch a taxi, he gets stopped by two policemen.

"Sir, are you Gilberto Landa?" says one of the police officers.

"Yes. Can I help you with something?" replies Gilberto, with a strong accent, wanting to sound like an innocent tourist.

"We are curious to find out what is the operation currently taking place in the presidential suite," claims the officer.

"Oh, we are just a group of friends planning a potential new venture. Is there a problem?" asks Gilberto.

"Not unless you're creating one. Can we take a look?" asks the officer.

"Sure, but for sake of confidentiality, I just need to let our lawyers know first, is that ok?" Gilberto knows that holding the officers back might bring suspicions. So, he pretends to text with an attorney, but instead spends about a minute writing to Phil, explaining that police officers might enter the room soon.

Phil gets on immediate alert. Where could he hide the money, ledgers, and computer? He instructs Bianca and the Raptors to bring all the evidence to the master bedroom. He removes a large painting from the wall and starts softly knocking on the drywall to determine how much hollow space is available. Probably enough to hide most of the incriminating evidence. He opens up a hole in the drywall with a knife, starts throwing stacks of money inside and asks the Raptors to scurry around the suite to find tape to hold the drywall back in place afterwards. The stacks of money drop all the way to the bottom of the inside of the wall and will probably be hard to recover but Phil figures it's better than being found by the police. They are able to conceal all the money, but nothing else will fit. Phil tapes up the wall, puts the painting back in place and leaves the computer and paperwork scattered over a desk. He purposely makes it look disorganized and random, like a bunch of people hashing things out, rather than a highly tuned crime syndicate.

The officers enter the room, and Phil presses his emergency button to call the Enforcement Division. He immediately receives text messages from Tiago and explains the situation cryptically. Tiago instructs Phil to make as much small talk as possible with the officers until he arrives. However, the officers are in no mood for discussions. As they bring in sniffer dogs, Phil realizes that they seem to think that a drug operation was taking place in the suite. This is fairly good news because it may distract the officers from seeing what was actually going on. Phil is hoping, however, that no connection is made with his questioning at a Singapore hospital a few months ago; there is only so many times that someone can escape suspicions from police officers.

Tiago arrives at the suite within minutes, dressed in a security guard uniform and addresses the officers with authority.

"Officers, I am part of the hotel security and would like to understand the nature of your intervention," says Tiago.

"We apprehended a guest by the name of Gilberto Landa and enquired about his business in Singapore and more specifically in this hotel. We didn't find that his answers corroborated our surveillance intelligence and eye-witness reports, so we requested to that your guests voluntarily submit to a search," explains one of the officers.

"Well, sir, this is hotel property, and searches have to be approved by both guests and hotel management, unless, of course, you are in possession of a search warrant. There are other guests in the hotel, and we wouldn't want to create unnecessary panic or unsubstantiated need to affect the serenity of clients' stay with us. I am sure that you can appreciate the potential negative impact that this could bring to our business – it would only take one quick picture on social media," says Tiago with the utmost authority.

"We understand," replies the officer.

"In this case, we do not see any justification for your alarming presence on our premises," concludes Tiago.

The officers leave quietly. Phil is surprised at how articulate and well-prepared Tiago was in his interaction with the police. He must have done this before.

Phil confers with Gilberto and reaches Ernesto over phone. Setting a proper office for the new company is now urgent. They can no longer work in a public place. Ernesto tasks the Legal Team with finding a top-notch office space in Singapore, which will be secured from authorities and sumptuous enough to attract the best talent.

Chapter 15

After two months operating from the Marina Bay Sands' presidential suite, the whole Equit organization is ready to move into its new fifty-thousand square-foot office in downtown Singapore, which includes three suites for executives to live directly in the office, a standard feature for most of Norrid's office locations. The employees hired so far will continue to stay in regular rooms of the Marina Bay Sands hotel until their families relocate to Singapore. Phil, Bianca, and Gilberto are checking out of the presidential suite today and will live in the office quarters for the time being.

The trio starts doing some back-and-forth between the hotel and the office, carrying important items themselves, thereby not risking a bell man handling or noticing confidential articles. As they travel through the lobby a few times, they observe significant police force and security guards. Phil decides to chat up the concierge to find out what is going on. It turns out that the Canadian Prime Minister is visiting tomorrow, and security preparations are underway. He will actually check into the presidential suite, so the concierge reminds Phil that they will need to check out as soon as possible, so that housekeeping can finalize the arrangements in the room for the Prime Minister's official visit.

With all the security eyes on people going in and out of the hotel, Phil tells Gilberto that they cannot carry the remaining cash out of the room. And since they have to check out of the suite, they will need to seal the remaining approximately $6 million of cash into the wall of the suite. They head out to a convenience store and buy 12 tubes of industrial grade caulk sealant. Back to the room, they glue the painting over the hole that they had opened up for storage of the cash. Someone would have to severely damage the painting to access the hole and given who is the next guest in the suite, Phil is confident that the painting will be intact. They will have to book the room again in a few days to collect the money.

Now that Phil and Bianca have some privacy again, settled in an executive suite within the office perimeters, Phil attempts to mend the relationship.

"Am I imagining, or you seem to have gained some interest in helping us to setup Equit?" asks Phil.

"Yes, I must admit that I feel some level of excitement in having broad responsibilities over the structure and administration of the fund. And Equit itself is not an illegal operation, so I don't see myself as a criminal. You, however, ..." Bianca says jokingly.

"Ah... soon, you'll be just as guilty as me. What about life on the edge and living like rock stars?" asks Phil.

"I don't consider myself a 'high-maintenance' type, but the luxurious life in top hotels, private jet, etc, is hard to ignore," replies Bianca.

"So, you don't completely dislike me anymore?" says Phil with a romantic smile, as he gets closer to Bianca and attempts holding her hand.

"Not so fast, cowboy... you've been demoted to roommate until you prove your value to me again," says Bianca with a broad smile on her face, which Phil interprets as a temporary suspension of their relationship status with improving chances of getting back on track very soon.

With the office now properly setup and dozens of employees already hired, funds under management grow rapidly from the laundering activities across many countries. Bianca begins interacting with the accounting teams of the shareholders of Equit. She is in close contact with Norrid's Ostriches based in Singapore and the Corporate Financial Reporting team of Goang based in Hong Kong.

Goang requires extensive financial information with frequent filings of spreadsheets and forms back to their office. Bianca complains to Phil that she will have to hire a whole accounting crew, not only to deal with the demands of Equit's business, but also to meet the extensive needs of Goang. They decide to call the Financial Controller of Goang to attempt to find a compromise between meeting their hunger for financial information and having to setup a massive accounting operation infrastructure in Singapore – primarily for Goang's needs.

Only minutes into the conversation with Goang's representatives, Phil and Bianca's hearts stop when it is revealed that Goang's request for information is because the company is listed on the Hong Kong stock exchange. Phil immediately recognizes that this is a massive problem. Listed companies not only publish information about their activities to public shareholders and securities commissions, but they are subject to heightened standards of governance, audit, regulations, etc.

Phil's next call is to chew out Li aggressively. How could he possibly think that linking a listed company to a money laundering operation was a good idea? The expected swift growth of Equit is going to bring so much attention to both Goang and Equit, that it is risking detection and possible prosecution of everyone involved. Li's name, of course, is not mentioned anywhere in the incorporation papers of Equit, nor is he mentioned as an officer, so he is much more relaxed about the matter. He may even be able to completely deny knowing about Equit's questionable source of funds. Phil regrets not investigating Goang beforehand, but then again, he was stuck in Li's captivity when Equit was being setup.

Phil decides to conference in Ernesto to help fix this before it's too late. However, Ernesto is not very knowledgeable with the governance aspects of corporations and public markets, so he tells Phil that he is not worried about the matter. Moreover, Li pushes back very strongly against any suggestion to make changes to the corporate structure in place. In fact, he argues that changes could bring undue attention. Finally, Li even contends that the very point that Phil is bringing up could be used to further hide the questionable sources of funds since authorities would assume that since Goang is listed, its governance would preclude any illegal activity and therefore Equit would be less on the radar of investigators. Phil becomes very sarcastic in the conversation to clearly highlight the flaws of this reverse logic. Ernesto interrupts him, concludes that the setup will remain and orders everyone to go back to work.

Phil and Bianca convene in an office to debrief. They are devastated by the developments. More than ever, they need an exit plan and make sure that their names do not appear anywhere. As they start listing out all the corporate documents, meetings, processes, or other items that they need to extract themselves from, a sudden loud banging starts on the door. Phil's heart rate shoots up as he turns around, and sees Tiago enter the room. Phil's usual fear of Tiago is palpable.

"You need to get the cash back from the presidential suite at the Marina Bay Sands Hotel," says Tiago.

"Ya, you wish. I'll explain to you where it is and how to get it out, so that you can get it," replies Phil, with a smart attitude. He is already putting in practice his extraction from risky activities.

"You created the mess, and even glued an expensive painting over the hole. How do you expect me to retrieve the money?" asks Tiago.

"Your big muscles obviously drained all the energy from your brain. The wall is hollow. You just need to pull out the bed, make a new hole near the ground and the money will easily come out. Then you put the bed back in place and everything is covered," explains Phil, with a tone that would be used by a kindergarten teacher.

"If you're so smart, you're coming with me," Tiago says with authority.

"It's called segregation of duties. I handle financial transactions, not ground operations. If you're not happy with your assigned responsibilities, take it up with your boss. I take directions from Ernesto, not you. Now get out of here, we have work to do," says Phil as he closes the door.

Phil continues to be quite troubled with Goang's listed status. He decides to have a meeting with Dr. Debo, the former professor who heads the Chameleons' department. Phil explains to him Goang's public status and involvement as a joint venture partner in Equit. Dr. Debo immediately understands Phil and Bianca's concern and agrees that Goang's extensive information disclosures will expose Equit, and the rest of Norrid, by forcing explanations of how all the unusual profits are generated. This undue attention will undoubtedly happen as soon as Goang publishes increased profitability from its investment in Equit and its stock price will be propelled to levels significantly higher.

Further research into Goang's activities reveals that the company manufactures and assembles parts of telecom and other electronic equipment in Hong Kong as well as other parts of southern China. Their sales to mobile phones companies based in countries around the world have stagnated over the past years, primarily due to global geo-political events. Dr. Debo concludes that even the slightest increase in Goang's revenues and profitability will have to be explained, and its disclosures will need to mention Equit within just a few short months from now.

Given the nature of Goang's operations, Dr. Debo believes that it would be best to construct an investment story within Equit, which would be in the space of electronics or virtual services, so that investors and regulators would not see this sudden profitability as completely disjointed from the rest of Goang. In other words, Equit's books and records would need to be falsified to make people believe that a large share of Equit's investments relate to activities and industries alike those of Goang's.

After initially disagreeing to be part of a scheme to falsify the accounting ledgers, Bianca realizes that her own security is at risk, and fixing this problem might be her only recourse. So, she suggests to Phil and Dr. Debo, that they should falsify cryptocurrency trades. Her proposal is to hire a few knowledgeable traders who might bring legitimacy to the entire operation. But in addition to the lawful trades, the Chameleons would produce fake trade evidence that would appropriate trades to Equit. While trades are visible on the records of the cryptocurrency blockchain ledgers, a lot of players use pseudonyms, so Equit could easily support to auditors that certain trades were made by its traders under unknown pseudonyms.

Dr. Debo is very impressed with Bianca's idea as cryptocurrencies are close enough to Goang's business, and the fake profitable trades could absorb large amounts of cash coming in from the currency booths. Essentially hitting two birds with one stone. He recommends that a Raptor impersonates a cryptocurrency trader, to whom they would allocate the fake profitable trades. Dr. Debo tells Phil that he will have the Chameleons start immediately on researching what cryptocurrency trade documents look like, and a process to produce large numbers of fake trades. Finally, Bianca recommends that a Raptor also joins the accounting department in order to match up money coming in from the booths' operations to the crypto trades. A regular accountant cannot be tasked with this.

The trio is quite happy with their plan and decide to update Ernesto, who presents no objection.

Phil is very proud of Bianca for her initiative and brilliance. He is also secretly hoping that her further involvement with the darker side of Norrid will keep her happy for as long as they are under the grip of Ernesto, and perhaps allow to rekindle their romantic relationship.

Phil debriefs Alex Nood, the newly hired manager in charge of Equit's currency trading, about plans to initiate cryptocurrency transactions, which will be under his supervision. Phil faces resistance. Alex has a Type A personality, very confident, hyper-active and trained on Wall Street with the most ruthless cutthroat traders in the world. He is used to deal with complicated businesses and organizations. Being, and more importantly looking, in command in front of his colleagues and team members is crucial.

Therefore, Alex will not let a bureaucrat like Phil dictate how he should do his job and the types of assets that he needs to trade, especially given the volatility and risks associated with cryptocurrencies. Alex is concerned that this marginal trading will be a distraction and provide low profitability, potentially even generate losses that Alex would become responsible for. Over several hours of meetings, Phil tries everything to convince him, including an intellectual lecture from Dr. Debo and an emotional, almost flirtatious, plea from Bianca. Nothing works. Alex is hardheaded. Phil cannot rely on Alex's discretion, and therefore cannot reveal to him the purpose and plans for the fake trades.

Phil, Bianca, and Dr. Debo reconvene and agree to find the fake crypto Raptor trader to be hired by Equit, and falsify a trading performance history, from a different made-up employer, that would convince Alex of the potential profits. Over the following few days, the Chameleons prepare documents showing the profile of Jack Frey, the Raptor identified for the mission, his performance of the prior three years and reference contact information, which would be answered by other Raptors if Alex were to actually check the references.

A week after their initial argument about cryptocurrencies, now armed with a thick dossier, Phil connects with Alex once again.

"Hey, can I talk to you for a minute?" asks Phil.

"Look, we're busy dealing with real transactions. I don't have time for your fantasies," replies Alex without even looking at Phil and with the condescending tone of the overconfident person that he is.

"I have something to show you, which I'm sure you're going to like," offers Phil.

"I'll give you five minutes. This better not be another waste of my time," says Alex as he slowly gets up, his eyes still glued to monitors showing various market information. They walk together to a conference room. Alex turns to his co-workers, raises his eyebrows, smiles, and shakes his head. Phil can hear five or six people laughing in his back as he closes the door of the room.

"We found Jack Frey, a crypto trader with an impressive performance track record, which we checked with his previous employer," announces Phil as he hands over the file. Alex carefully scans through the records for several minutes.

"Is this really all legit? asks Alex.

"We checked everything. We even called their external auditors," lies Phil.

"This is indeed impressive. Listen, if I agree to let this guy join our desk, twenty five percent of his profits need to be distributed as bonus to my team members in the manner that I will dictate," says Alex. Clearly asking for an unusual arrangement to divert a big portion of the crypto trading profitability to himself and a select few.

"This shouldn't be a problem. I'll clear this with management," says Phil, confident he will be able to convince Ernesto. And Phil doesn't care too much about over-paying people, as long as revenues from crypto trading can be somewhat associated with Goang's activities to create sufficient divergence from Equit's inflows. Phil hopes, however, that the compensation of Equit's traders and analysts doesn't have to be disclosed in Goang's public filings.

Chapter 16

Both Ernesto and Li surprisingly spend an increasing amount of time in Equit's office. They seem to enjoy the energy of the startup, especially that new personnel coming in everyday are delighted with the conditions and benefits from their employer. Phil finds it interesting to watch Ernesto and Li, who work for competing criminal organizations, cooperate and seem wholeheartedly trying to make this partnership work.

With Equit's structure in place and most of the employees hired, cash is pouring in fast, and as a result, investment and trading profits are already shooting up, especially in the currency trading division. The Chameleons can barely keep up with the fake crypto trades doctoring to match the cash that's coming in at an increasing pace, especially from Li's operations, overtaking Norrid's share. The partners now look more like 60%-40%. Phil knew this could happen but didn't expect it to be that quick. To avoid conflicts between the partners, Phil instructs Gilberto to integrate a more balanced amount of cash from each partner, so that the split doesn't further tip in favor of Goang.

This implies, however, that Li's cash integration will slow down and will have to be stored somewhere. Phil asks the

Enforcement Division of Norrid to setup a safe location in Singapore or Kuala Lumpur to hold cash waiting for integration.

In order to avoid attention from the growing profitability of Equit, Bianca uses her thorough knowledge of the accounting ledgers to suggest to Phil that they should book more expenses to reduce the profits. They brainstorm ideas for a few minutes, with the objective of finding a way to spend more without literally throwing money out the window.

- Paying a special welcome bonus to the employees in exchange for a retention agreement, which would also ensure their loyalty to Equit for a period of time.
- Rent more office space, paid by Equit but made available to Norrid and Goang's other businesses. This could be done in any city where those businesses operate.
- Buy products and services from Norrid and Goang's businesses that may or may not be necessary to run Equit's operations.
- Take over an unprofitable company, thereby diluting profits, and provide scale to Equit for expansion at a later stage.

When they discuss those ideas with Dr. Debo, he expresses that only the special bonus really makes a difference. The office space and products purchasing ideas would otherwise improve Goang's profitability, which would anyway alert investors. Also, it could alert Goang's management that something dodgy might be going on at Equit. As far as taking over a company that is running at a loss, Dr. Debo believes that the announcement of such acquisition would attract attention in and of itself, and probably require various governance procedures with Goang. Their management and board would need to be convinced that the potential target is viable and accretive, in the long run, to Goang's shareholders.

Therefore, they all agree to go with a special employee bonus. The initial bonus will be disbursed to employees, six to eight weeks after their hiring. Given that the employees were steadily hired over a few months, the expense will be staggered over a certain time, thereby slowing Equit's increasing profitability during its first year of operation.

Employees are in euphoria when this gets announced. They receive money to agree to stay in a job for which they already loved the generous benefits. No brainer. If any of the employees knew the full extent of the criminal activities cover-up associated with this sudden benefit, perhaps the reaction would be different.

Phil and Bianca shift their attention back to Goang. They hold several conference calls with their Investor Relations department in order to ensure that disclosures, information and messaging to external parties are in line with the cryptocurrency story of Equit. Phil goes out of his way to convince Goang's representatives that crypto trading is by far the single largest contributor of Equit's profits and is largely in line with Goang's industry. A few executives of Goang jump on the bandwagon to claim that part of crypto success story is due to their strategic thinking, planning and flawless execution. Phil loves the reaction and smiles at their hunger for cowardly taking credit for Equit's success.

With its otherwise steady business, Goang's stock price has been hovering around HK$8, approximately US$1, for the past two years. In August, Goang publishes its quarterly financial information, which for the first time, includes its share of Equit's profits. Markets are pleased with Goang's increasing profitability, but analysts that closely follow the stock believe that the relatively small increase is due to an unusual trading gain and therefore episodic, in other words, it would not reproduce in the future. They advise their clients to be cautious. The stock picks up some volume and moves to a respectable HK$9.

Phil breathes a sigh of relief. Despite Equit being mentioned publicly by Goang, alarm bells will not go off until the profitability increases further. Phil, Bianca, and Dr. Debo seem to be the only ones seeing the upcoming train wreck though – which could be as soon as next quarter. The profit reduction measures implemented by giving bonuses to employees will soon wear off. They'll have to think of something else.

Employees of Equit take pride in the success of Goang, which they feel part of. Phil is in complete disbelief as Li and Ernesto do a victory parade around the office and distribute high-fives to Alex's team. The floor starts shaking when the staff suddenly stomp their feet on the ground, and call for a speech by Alex, who initially declines out of made-up modesty. But after a few seconds, he moves to the middle of the trading floor, and raises his hands as if he just threw a touchdown pass. He starts his address to the staff by thanking and congratulating everyone for their hard work to setup of Equit. While recounting how his insights in the world of cryptocurrencies had led him to find a superstar in Jack Frey, Alex's eyes move around the crowd. He definitely avoids locking eyes with Phil though. Alex is really believing his own lies. Phil just wonders how this will look when it all crumbles.

With everyone seemingly in a festive mood, applauding Alex as their new leader, Phil and Bianca stand in the back of the room, their elbows rested on a filing cabinet, slightly touching and looking at each other with an amorous grin, happy to be outside of any limelight that may be subject to investigations down the road. For all his pride and ego, Alex has no idea of the risks associated with taking responsibility for generating all this fake profit. Phil turns to Bianca with a satisfied smile and suggests that they go to Bali for the weekend to see the apartment that he bought a few months ago. This short journey might also give them a chance to design other profit reduction schemes, or even better: develop an exit plan.

Chapter 17

George, the developer in Bali, is glad to finally meet Phil. He had started to wonder if the buyer of the most expensive unit of the new building would ever show up. They walk around the property, equipped with amenities usually available in expensive resorts: infinity pools, gym overlooking the Bali sea, beach service available to owners and a pool-side bar. Before they even see the inside of their unit, Bianca is already thinking that this could be their hiding spot.

George tours the interior of the three thousand square-foot luxurious apartment, sporting three large bedrooms, a massive living room, a gourmet kitchen equipped with the latest technologies, and a sound-proof meditation room connected to the balcony with a breath-taking view over the water. George had some rented furniture delivered for Phil and Bianca so they could occupy the apartment immediately, and he warns Phil about the strict rules limiting his ability to lease out the place to tenants. In other words, if his intent were to consider this apartment as an investment, the returns would be dismal. George's words hang in the air for a few seconds as Phil gets distracted for a moment, wondering whether dismal investment returns on certain assets could help him solve part of the problem with Equit.

After George leaves, Bianca jumps into Phil's arms.

"Please tell me that nobody at Norrid is aware of this place?" asks Bianca with a charming smile.

"Sorry darling, Ernesto found out, somehow. They really have their fingers everywhere. It's extremely difficult to know which lawyer or banker to trust. Norrid's operatives are always two steps ahead. People end up getting bought out by the extensive means of our favorite criminal organization," explains Phil. Bianca is disappointed. Phil doesn't know how to turn this topic back to where she was smiling, so he quickly switches the conversation to Equit. "Hey, George just made me think of something. Could we fake trade losses on certain investments in order to reduce Equit's earnings?" asks Phil.

"Yes, but we would need to place the 'lost' money somewhere. It would be like defrauding Equit and, as a result, making that money illegal again, essentially reversing what the currency booths have done to launder the money," says Bianca.

"Yeah, you're right," replies Phil, thinking of his years of corporate fraud, diverting money all over the world. "It wouldn't help or be productive for the shareholders of Equit."

"And similarly, actual trading losses (i.e., purposely losing money) wouldn't be well perceived by the shareholders after all the trouble of laundering it. And the employees of Equit wouldn't go along since their bonuses would be lost," concludes Bianca. Phil nods.

Phil takes advantage of this time away from Norrid's potential surveillance to catch up with Antonio, his attorney from Brazil, to get an update on the yacht purchase. Antonio confirms that he placed an order on a refurbished yacht that is currently in the Caribbean Sea and is making arrangements to have it sailed to South East Asia. Phil stops him and tells him to arrange for the yacht to be delivered to the Bahamas, and then wait for his instructions. Phil thinks that with his jet, he might actually be able to reach it quicker if he needed. Sailing the yacht across the world might take weeks.

Phil and Bianca have become used to anonymity and seclusion given the nature of their work with Norrid and Equit. So, they are taken aback when an American couple, Paul and Linda, approaches them while they are bathing in the complex's pool. They could be just being friendly, or Paul could be wishing to take a closer look at Bianca in her hot bikini.

Paul sports a small beer belly and is mostly bald, but looks good despite being in his sixties, and probably five to ten years older than Linda, who is visibly well pampered. However, she looks like she might have been through too many plastic surgeries, and perhaps had extended exposure to the sun or tanning beds.

Phil is still on his guards and provides limited information about himself and keeps turning the conversation back on them. The two couples end up having drinks at the bar for a few hours. Around eight o'clock, Paul declares that it's time for dinner and wants Phil and Bianca to come up to their apartment to share an enormous roast beef that their personal chef has been slow cooking since mid-afternoon. Bianca, already tipsy immediately accepts, clearly lacking social interaction in her new corporate life at Equit.

Upon entering their apartment, Phil instantly sees that Paul's previously announced retirement must have been at the expense of someone else's hard work. Although the floor space is about half of Phil's penthouse, the apartment is like a museum of art and precious metals. The marble, rich oak furniture and trims must be worth millions.

"So, Paul, what kind of business were you in?" asks Phil.

"Oh, the last time I did any kind of useful work was one hour before the dot com bubble burst in 2000. I was no prophet. I just exchanged all my holdings of internet stocks into cash that day, ready to go on a holiday. I've haven't been back to the financial markets since," explains Paul.

"That was a well-timed holiday. How have you kept busy all these years?" continues Phil.

"Just buying real estate and precious collections, as you can see. I came across this beautiful property by the water, but unfortunately someone had already snatched up the penthouse," replies Paul. Phil just nods and move his eyebrows as he continues to withhold information from Paul while giving his approval for the exquisite pieces of art.

"Oh, that would be us!" Shouts Bianca from across the room. Phil smiles at the thought of Bianca clearly identifying herself as a couple with him by making it sound like they own the property together. However, she is more than tipsy now. Phil has never seen her that way. She might divulge way too much if she keeps drinking.

"No way... you didn't," says Paul, with both a smile and jealous tone. "Can we see it?"

"We just moved in yesterday with rented furniture, nothing exciting," replies Phil.

"And we might have to kill you if you know where we live," adds Bianca, continuing in her mix of happiness and letting her guards down a little too much. Phil gives her a quick dirty look.

"In that case, we really need to see it," says Paul with a loud laugh.

The four of them take the elevator to the penthouse and open the door. Phil almost has a heart attack when he sees someone on the balcony. It's Tiago again. He comes into the room and introduces himself to Paul and Linda. Phil introduces Tiago as his driver and tells him "you can go back to the car now, thank you", which he does. Bianca gives a reproaching look to Phil for his rude comment in front of their guests. She then turns to Paul and Linda to start walking around the apartment.

After a few minutes, they return to Paul's apartment to continue their dinner and social evening. Bianca keeps drinking and slips increasingly dangerous statements about the nature of their criminal activities, which Phil tries to laugh off as ridiculous. Linda seems a good sport and cracks some jokes around Bianca's revelations, and it somewhat smooths off the effect. Paul, however, becomes really interested in some of the details, which makes Phil very uncomfortable.

"In all seriousness though, I've always wondered how criminal gangs were able to run global operations, and move so much money without getting caught," says Paul, tightening his lips and moving his head left to right, looking very pensive. Phil knows that Paul is being inquisitive, border line suspicious.

"Until they do get caught. But yeah, I don't know. It's a world that we need to steer clear of. So, I guess we'll never know," says Phil.

"I think sometimes good people get drawn into dangerous territories, for one reason or another, and they find innovative ways to extract themselves from trouble," says Bianca before taking another sip of wine and winking at Phil.

"I guess it's possible. I'm just happy that we don't have to be anywhere near these awful crimes," lies Phil, as he gets up and starts examining Paul's art collection to force a clean break in the conversation.

Thirty minutes later, when the topic shifts to fashion and shopping, Phil is able to safely escape for a few minutes to connect with Tiago in the basement's parking lot.

"What were you thinking to come over here? You're putting us all in great danger," says Phil, as Tiago opens the door to let him in a car for a conversation.

"We've been trying to reach you for 24 hours. Li is furious and we need you to calm him down. If I didn't come here, he would have sent his guys, and you would be tied up to something uncomfortable right now," says Tiago in a soft but firm tone.

"What is the problem?" asks Phil.

"He says that you are favoring Norrid in the integration of cash and that you've purposely slowed down the growth of Equit. Both of which are apparently hurting Goang. Nobody knows what he's talking about," explains Tiago. Phil knows exactly what this is about and actually not far from the truth.

"Ok, I'll call him right now," says Phil.

Phil calls Li and clarifies that Goang has not lost anything and explains that he saw as his job to ensure a gradual undetected growth for Equit and harmony between the partners, which would protect the long term interests of everyone.

"You have no idea what you're talking about. If we wanted harmony, we would have hired a preacher, and we wouldn't need you as our money laundering specialist," says Li, with a tone that could petrify the most confident person.

"Listen, it's important that..." says Phil before being interrupted.

"You don't get to decide what's important. You work for us. Let me make it abundantly clear to you. Your physical well-being is fully dependent on your ability to crank your money laundering machine at maximum speed and unleash as much growth as possible for Equit," explains Li.

"With all due respect Li, we need to operate in a way to remain undetected, so we need to exercise some restraint," says Phil, lowering his voice given Li's threats.

"You're still not listening. Do as I say. And remember, at this point of the implementation, the scheme is running well, and eliminating you would not make much difference for Equit's partners," says Li, then hangs up.

Now Phil is worried. He actually agrees with Li's statement about his somewhat limited value at this point. Now that Equit is up and running, Phil's contribution is far less than it had been, and he may have to rely on the likes of Tiago for Bianca and himself to remain alive. Moreover, Li's organization might start to follow Phil's every move, further limiting his movements and increasing the need for security.

Phil rejoins the group. He spends the rest of the evening avoiding questions in addition to thwarting the many embarrassments created by Bianca becoming an open book with the increasing effect of alcohol.

Bianca is hungover and has a massive headache upon awaking on Sunday morning. Phil was planning to give her a hard time about her comments to Paul and Linda, but decides to let it go for now, in order to focus on the latest priority. He now needs another solution to prove to Ernesto, and possibly Li that he and Bianca are still crucial to Equit.

Chapter 18

Back to Singapore, Phil, Bianca and Dr. Debo huddle in a conference room to discuss the challenge now facing them. Just one month into the quarter, Equit's performance and growth seems exponential, especially for the crypto desk. Dr. Debo hands data over to Phil showing that the trading volume and share price of Goang is picking up to abnormal levels. The market seems to like Goang, despite its sluggish core business.

Phil shares his idea of purposely getting Equit into unprofitable trades, generating a strong opposition from Bianca, primarily because funds would need to be fraudulently diverted from Equit, which she wants no part of. Dr. Debo agrees that a fraud scheme is risky in the circumstances, it could even be detected by Goang's Internal Audit department, which is scheduled to review Equit's operations in the near future. And who knows whether Li would start sniffing around or get a tip from an employee of Equit, potentially angering him to the point of threatening lives.

However, Dr. Debo asks whether Equit could enter into high risk trades to buy shares issued by companies subject to significant lawsuits or being reviewed by government agencies for presumably having damaged the environment, for example. While the outcome of such events could turn either way, there is a chance that it turns into a large loss.

After further research, Dr. Debo narrows down a list of potential targets to:

• Three cigarette makers that are being sued by various governments with verdicts expected over the next few months;
• Four chemical and fertilizer conglomerates subject to class action lawsuits for pollution; and,
• Three pharmaceutical companies in the final stages of critical drug reviews with the US Food and Drug Administration ("FDA").

How is that for uncertainty? After debating the risk profile of each candidate, they zero in on Biotyla, a research and technology company with a cancer drug under review. Market analysts believe that given the level of debt and no other promising project, they would have to file for bankruptcy if the FDA were to turn down their drug. The outcome should be known within a few weeks.

Phil suggests that Dr. Debo mobilizes the Chameleons to make up a research report that strongly recommends that investors buy Biotyla stock and fabricate quotes of a high chance of approval following information received from a knowledgeable company insider. Bianca freezes every time Phil's mind turns to evil plans. This time though, she agrees that they need to go ahead with this plan.

A few days later, the research report is ready. Since Phil made Alex rich and famous with the crypto trading, he turns to him again to discuss Biotyla, hoping to influence his greedy but weak mind with another fabricated opportunity. Despite being a currency trader, perhaps using Alex's new popularity to sway others would be a workable strategy.

"Hey Alex, a friend of mine sent me something, which has not yet been published, and I wanted to get your thoughts," says Phil in an innocent tone.

"Sure thing Phil. What is it?" asks Alex, now more inclined to listen to Phil's ideas.

"Have you heard of Biotyla? Apparently, they are just about to receive approval for a game changing cancer drug. My buddy gave me this report that's going to be published next week. I know you're into currencies, but can you give this a look for me to see if we should invest?" asks Phil, in a nonchalant way, giving the impression that it's an unimportant piece of paper.

"Alright, I'll read it tonight," answers Alex.

Phil observes from a distance as Alex's curiosity drove him to immediately read the report. Then, he suddenly jumps from his seat and walks over to an analyst that covers biotech stocks. The two of them spend 20 minutes carefully reviewing the report and smile widely at each other. Minutes later, they put an order on the market for 200,000 shares at $30. The order will go through as soon as the New York Stock Exchange opens.

Phil, Bianca and Dr. Debo huddle again. Phil recommends a second phase for this plan, this time more diabolical: send an anonymous letter to the Head of the FDA, raising public safety concerns with Biotyla's proposed drug. Dr. Debo smiles at the ingenuity. Bianca is not happy.

Chapter 19

Henry Dylerman is a third generation American-Irish born in a rich family. His father had been a coffee importer and trader, before becoming the CEO of the New York Stock Exchange in the 1970's. Henry grew up attending the best private schools in New York City, dining at the most exclusive clubs and meeting distinguished guests at his parents' sumptuous apartment on Park Avenue. His father had instilled in him a work ethic discipline that led to Honors degrees from Harvard and Yale.

So, it came at no surprise to anyone when KexCorp Industries, the 200 years old conglomerate, appointed Henry as its Chairman and CEO in 2002 at the age of only 35. He had accumulated so much knowledge from public companies' filings and daily interrogation of his father since he was a boy, that he could navigate the financial markets with instinct and flair. Traits that all business leaders wished they possessed, in a world driven by pre-packaged management methods and decisions made by data models.

The years immediately following the two major disruptions of the early twenty-first century, 9/11 and the Global Financial Crisis, have been the most fruitful for Henry and KexCorp. He has used the vast resources of

KexCorp to take advantage of low stock prices during both of these periods to scoop up hundreds of companies of all sizes and in every industry.

Henry is also the champion of strong governance, culture and ethics for all businesses and government bodies operating in the greater New York City area. He is a frequent speaker at industry conferences and luncheons, to advocate that good and transparent practices in the financial markets bring the best returns for everyone. During internal KexCorp meetings, he calls out any attempt from his executives at obscuring or embellishing the truth. He lectures them about the importance of sound practice. "Let good ethical behavior guide you", he would always say to his staff, like a robot stuck on repeat.

In the mid-90s, while still a mid-level executive, Henry had been responsible for campus recruitment of associates. Amongst others, he had hired Phil in 1997, and Josh, in 1998. Henry had seen in Phil a keen ability to manage complicated processes and integrate operations of acquired companies. Josh, on the other hand, had stayed very close to Henry through his progression to the top of the company, as a special advisor, especially as it relates to target companies that Kexcorp should be looking at acquiring.

Phil and Josh had always been on good terms but also under a continuous competition to determine who was the most successful. Phil had always seen Josh as kissing up to the boss and getting Kexcorp into transactions that Phil had to clean up afterwards. Josh always made fun of Phil for being a complaining bureaucrat. When Phil "retired", Josh initially felt some sort of victory. But also felt a sense that Phil had achieved his dream prior to him. That bothered Josh.

It bothered Josh even more that Henry was devastated when Phil handed his resignation. Henry would have taken it better if Phil had left for a competitor, perhaps even giving a chance to Henry to outbid with new salary and conditions. A retirement at a young age made Henry feel like Phil had been fed up with conditions at KexCorp. And this didn't reflect well on Henry and the company.

On a quiet summer weekend day, Henry relaxes on the balcony of his Park Avenue apartment. He is catching up on newspapers of the past few days. A small article catches his attention. An unknown company listed on the Hong Kong Stock Exchange is the star of the week in terms of price increase and growth of traded volume. Goang had just made its way to Henry's mind. He immediately emails Josh to look into the company, its main business, key executives and most importantly, what could possibly bring abnormal volume to the stock. Something must be brewing.

Josh, the overachiever, gets on to the task immediately. He mobilizes a team of analysts to review the past three years of Goang's public filings, build extensive profiles of its senior management and model which direction the stock would go over the next few months.

On Monday morning, Josh meets Henry to present a 20-page report on Goang, detailing its simple and stable operations. Nothing too new or exciting except of course the recent investment in Equit, which has a foray into cryptocurrencies. Josh adds that Equit's hire of some of the most prominent analysts, investors and traders had been mentioned in the news a few months ago, but nobody on Wall Street seem to have paid much attention.

Henry wonders why the market would have such an interest in what seemingly looks like a lucky trading gain by a joint venture investment of Goang. Nevertheless, he instructs Josh to start quietly building an ownership position in Goang, but to remain below 5% of the total shares outstanding. Henry insists that knowledge of the position, inside and outside KexCorp, must be extremely limited. If anyone became aware that KexCorp has an interest in Goang, the stock price would increase before Henry could even determine if Goang's long term prospects were viable. Henry has been in these types of situations dozens of times before. Absolute secrecy will offer KexCorp maximum flexibility.

Chapter 20

Equit's investment in Biotyla pays off big in less than a week. After the CEO of Biotyla appeared on MSNBC and stated he was confident that the FDA would approve their product, the stock doubles. A $6 million dollar gain for Equit.

Alex looks like a trading God, once again, for having come across information about Biotyla. Li assembles the employees for a celebration as service staff rolls in carts of expensive champagne. Alex's popularity with the staff is stratospheric. Everyone is thinking about their Christmas bonus and browsing through the websites of exotic cars and beach houses.

Phil is furious. The plan so far has gone in the exact opposite direction that it needed. He storms into Dr Debo's office and closes the door behind him.

"How are we doing with the letter to the FDA? We really need to hurry. For all we know, Li might make them sell the shares of Biotyla, and crystallize the gain," says Phil, in a complete panic.

"The letter is almost ready; it will go out tomorrow. But you really need to calm down. Your demeanor could bring suspicions from Li. You need to look like you're happy about the development. Perhaps you should even be the one to recommend looking into selling the investment given the price increase. Wait a few days and call a meeting with Li and some of the analysts to request a review into whether Equit should take some money off the table on Biotyla," recommends Dr. Debo.

"That sounds good, thank you," concludes Phil.

The anonymous letter to the FDA goes unanswered for two weeks. Phil is wondering whether the right people at the agency have even seen the letter. He decides to reconvene with Dr. Debo and recommends to send a copy of the letter to the New York Times and the Wall Street Journal – that will force the FDA to seriously consider it, or at least delay its process for some time. Although Dr. Debo is starting to feel uneasy about the extent of deception surrounding the Biotyla investment, he agrees that Equit's profit are way too high and the upcoming attention from the markets could lead to a massive police inquiry.

The letter is sent to the newspapers and Phil concurrently calls a meeting with Alex, Li as well as analysts and traders covering the Biotyla position. If the news hit immediately, the team will be in a conference room, wasting precious minutes to sell the stock.

"Given the increase in Biotyla's share price, should we think about selling out?" asks Phil. Everyone is looking at him with blank faces.

"Excuse-me, what is your expertise in this?" asks one of the analysts.

"Let's all keep a level head here. Phil is asking the right question. Look, I think this is just the beginning for Biotyla. Now that Biotyla has quasi-certainty of FDA approval, the stock will shoot up again once the product starts selling," says Alex.

"Are there research papers available to support this, Alex? Perhaps Phil is right, let's not be too greedy here," says Li. Phil is glad that Li noticed his recommendation, which might save some grief later when losses start mounting. However, selling immediately would actually be catastrophic for Phil. He needs to slow down the intentions to sell the stock.

"Everyone should sleep on this and think it over. Let's discuss in the morning," suggests Phil, hoping that the fabricated news is published in the meantime.

After everyone leaves for the night, Phil stays behind in a closed-door office. On his way out, he discreetly disconnects the computer monitor of the trader mainly responsible for the Biotyla position. That way, if news come out overnight, daytime in the U.S., and he wants to come in to execute a sale, he will be further delayed, potentially creating more losses for Equit.

When the newspapers finally start publishing that there might be safety issues with Biotyla's product, the stock swings wildly, but not providing the losses that Phil was hoping for. The movements are enough though for Alex and a few other analysts to come into the office during the night, Singapore time, to unload the position, realizing a net $4 million gain for Equit before Biotyla's stock starts to seriously tumble.

Phil finds out about the sale upon his arrival at the office in the morning. He congratulates the team, but he is fuming inside. He has not only failed to slow down the profitability of Equit but has made it even greater with the Biotyla trade. Frustrating to say the least.

Li, who has now seemed to set up his permanent work location in Equit's offices, approaches Phil.

"Phil, your flair continues to impress us every day, you have become such an important asset of our organization," says Li, with a tender smile.

"I'm just doing my job. I'm here to please the partners of Equit," replies Phil. Clearly nervous about where this conversation is going.

"You know, we always reward our best assets with the best benefits. So, once Equit is on cruise control, would you be ready for a new management challenge?" asks Li. This kind of comment makes Phil sick to his stomach. He sees exactly where Li is going with this and wonders whether these criminals will ever leave him alone.

"Ah, I've got enough challenges... And I thought my value was limited once Equit was set up," says Phil as he smiles and gently taps Li's shoulder, in reference to Li's latest threats. Phil's movements bring a dirty look from the security guard who is watching from across the floor.

"This was in the heat of the moment, Phil. I didn't mean it. I just wanted to ensure that Equit keeps growing steadily. I would like to negotiate your exit of Norrid with Ernesto in order for you to join me. What do you say?" asks Li.

"Ah, you know Li, if Norrid didn't need my services any longer, I would hope to retire in the sunset. I've had enough ulcers already," replies Phil, as softly as possible. His words hang in the air as he walks away from Li.

As if the Biotyla trade wasn't enough bad news for the day, now Li is planning a lifelong criminal career for Phil.

Today's problems just keep piling up. Gilberto informs Phil that cash inflows from Li's organization have increased again during the past few weeks and continue to be passed through the currency booths and on to the cryptocurrency scheme. But Norrid's inflows have all but dried up. Goang's share of Equit's profits is now at 70% and climbing.

What could be going on at Norrid to create cash flow issues? Has money started to be passed up again to Norrid's Corporate Treasury? Or are there more fundamental issues with Norrid's other divisions? Phil decides to huddle with Dr. Debo and Bianca to strategize on next steps. Dr. Debo reveals that the workload of the Chameleons has shifted to almost exclusively serve the crypto scheme. The demand for doctored paperwork from the legitimate businesses of Norrid around the world has reduced to almost nothing. And the most worrying part is that Dr. Debo was asked to produce documents to support the permanent closure of a few of Norrid's legitimate businesses.

A tale of two worlds. Each bringing a case of extreme worries for Phil. As if the incredible success of Goang wasn't enough to bring attention from the world, the sinking of Norrid would certainly bring its share of scrutiny.

After multiple attempts at reaching Ernesto, Phil decides that it is time to pay him a visit in person and brings Dr. Debo and Bianca along. They hop on the jet and head to Kuala Lumpur.

Their hope to surprise Ernesto in order to make him reveal what is going on with Norrid turns into a shock for the trio. The office is completely empty, except for the floor occupied by the Chameleons, who are hard at work to supply the crypto scheme. They do not know what happened to everyone else.

Phil checks out his office and opens his safe. His passports are all there, including his real one and the safe is full of money, from the weekly pay promised to him. The rest of the content seems untouched. Phil is surprised that Ernesto and his gang left without all this money. They must have been in a hurry. Or perhaps they'll be back soon with more work for Phil.

"Doctor, what do you suggest? Should we just take this opportunity to evade Norrid's grip?" asks Phil.

"Norrid has had ups and downs in the past. Whenever they find their footing again, they go after the people that lost their loyalty in the process. So, if you want to survive this, you should lay low and keep working as if nothing happened," answers Dr. Debo.

"What do you mean keep working? What exactly are we supposed to do now? Didn't we fulfill our mandate? Equit is up and running... what else?" asks Bianca, rather innocently.

"I guess it never ends with these types of organizations," replies Phil. "Where is Norrid's head office?" asks Phil as he turns towards Dr. Debo.

"On a few occasions over the years, we have worked on documents in French and German with addresses in Zurich, Switzerland. I would hypothesize that Norrid keeps cash there to benefit from the Swiss bank secrecy," explains Dr. Debo.

Despite deep curiosity about the fate of Norrid, Phil and Bianca decide to follow Dr. Debo's advice for the time being and hunker down in Phil's executive apartment in Kuala Lumpur.

Chapter 21

Equit's profitability has skyrocketed. Goang is about to have the best quarterly performance of its existence, with its share of the venture now standing at 80%, and its stock trading at HK$25 on much higher volume. Phil is no longer able to change the stock's trajectory. He knows that a wrecking ball of investigations is coming, and trying to intervene, once again, might backfire. Therefore, he convinces Bianca to pack everything and head to Jakarta. In his mind, staying away from any potential U.S. ally is better. Phil still doesn't have his valuable briefcase but has the fake passports, his own real passport and approximately $400,000 in cash, which he again hides under the mattress in the jet.

Upon arrival, in contrast to the last time that his jet was in Jakarta, Phil can easily obtain a hanger space. After sending Sergio and Claudio to a nearby hotel, he locks the hanger and gets settled to stay in the jet with Bianca for a few days.

With the announcement of its outsized financial performance, Goang's stock initially remains stable with limited volume. The analysts are digesting the complicated disclosures denoting large trading gains from Equit, the crypto currency dealings and the bizarre rise of Goang's relative shareholding of Equit during the period. Towards the end of the day in Asia, seemingly when the European markets reach midday and New York wakes up, the volume of Goang shares being exchanged picks up and the price hits a high of HK$70, only to retreat back to HK$62 on heavy selling during the last minutes before the closing bell.

The following morning, Phil's phone is buzzing at nine o'clock. Bruce Vankeg, the CEO of Goang is on the line. Phil has never met him but has been on a few conference calls with him, Ernesto and Li over the last few months. Bruce is desperately looking for Li.

"I haven't talked to Li for at least a week. I don't know where he is. I assume you've tried his cell phone and his office at Equit?" asks Phil.

"Yes. And no one has seen him for a few days," replies Bruce.

"Bummer, well, if I hear from him, I'll let him know to call you," says Phil, trying to end the conversation to avoid getting caught up in more dramas than he cares to handle.

"Well, perhaps you could help us. The authorities in Hong Kong contacted us last night to report unusual trading activity on our stock," inquires Bruce.

"What do you mean?" asks Phil. His heart rate shoots up as he's thinking about all the warnings he had given to Ernesto and Li.

"They said there was suspicious insider trading from Equit's employees on the Goang stock," explains Bruce.

Phil knows immediately what this means. Some employees of Equit knew, before everyone else in the market, that Goang was going to have a stellar profit, so they bought shares throughout the quarter and probably sold before the market closed yesterday. Which explains the volume and price increases during the quarter, before anyone else on the market had knowledge of the performance. With the price of Goang shares reacting positively upon the publication of the financial results, those Equit employees presumably sold shares in masses and created the small dip in the price at the end of the trading day.

"Well, I have not traded for my personal account in at least one year, so I'm not part of that. And I don't know of anyone that owned your stock recently. Sorry I can't help you more with this," says Phil. Clearly wanting to be excluded from this investigation.

"Alright, look, I don't know where this is going to lead, but I am guessing investigators will want to interview you and the rest of Equit's management," says Bruce.

"That's good because I am not part of Equit's management. I just helped with the setup. They're really going to have to speak to Li," concludes Phil.

Phil is not even sure who is officially the management of Equit – although it was managed by Ernesto and Li in practice over the past few months. Norrid's Legal Team must have put names of people when they created the company. Perhaps Ernesto? thinks Phil.

If insider trading is going to be the extent of the investigation, for which Phil wouldn't even be a target, that would be a great outcome, thinks Phil. If, however, this gives an opportunity for investigators to sniff around the crypto scheme, or worse, the source of Equit's funds, this could turn ugly.

A few days pass during which Phil and Bianca go back and forth between the jet and the airport terminal. Boredom starts settling in. A jet cabin is definitely not ideal for two people, and the tiny shower doesn't present the same intimate opportunities as the couple once had during their romantic trips.

Thinking of places that would allow them more space than an airplane, Phil wonders whether it would be a good opportunity to take possession of the penthouse that he bought in Jakarta. However, the place is unfurnished, and he doesn't know anyone that could help them determine whether strange visitors had come snooping around. In Bali though, they know Paul and Linda. Phil asks Bianca to call them and innocently ask whether they have seen anyone out of the ordinary on the premises.

Linda relates that all they saw were movers that came to pick up the rented furniture from Phil's apartment. But upon learning that Phil and Bianca were in Jakarta, Paul insists that they join them for a few days, and stay with them since their penthouse is now empty.

Phil calls Sergio and Claudio back to duty and they depart again. Upon landing in Bali, they are ordered by the airport's ground control to report to customs, despite their flight being domestic. Waiting for them at the designated parking area are six agents that seem less than friendly.

"Welcome to Bali. I'm Agent Dia with Interpol," says a tall, long hair brunette with a British accent, while flashing a police badge.

"Hi and thank you. We're kind of in a hurry. Can we talk another day?" says Phil while grabbing some luggage from the plane. He doesn't want to sound suspicious but also is not interested to join a conversation that he doesn't wish to have.

"We only have a few questions, and it would be in your best interest to listen to us," replies Agent Dia.

"What is this about?" asks Phil.

"We are investigating a possible insider trading scheme and believe that you may have valuable information for us," says the agent.

"Well, I don't currently have a brokerage account and haven't traded in years. Have you traded recently honey?" says Phil as he turns towards Bianca, who shakes her head 'no'.

"Actually, we are looking into transactions that originated from Equit's office in Singapore. We understand that you are associated with this firm," says Agent Dia, reaching for information.

"Well, we only provided a helping hand with the setup of Equit, so we cannot help with that either. Sorry," replies Phil.

"Sir, do you know Mr. Li?" asks Agent Dia.

"Yes, I have talked to him on a few occasions during the initial days of Equit," says Phil, trying to minimize any association with Li.

"Are you aware of Mr. Li's frequent trading of Goang's stock? And when he became aware of Equit's financial performance?" asks Agent Dia.

"I had no idea that he was a shareholder of Goang. And if you don't mind, I have some really important business to attend to, but I will definitely reach out to you if I come across additional information," says Phil as he walks away with Bianca and their luggage.

Phil now understands the last four months of his life. Li is turning out to be more brilliant and sophisticated than Phil had ever imagined. Li masterminded the purchase of significant amounts of Goang's stock throughout the whole time that Equit was ramping up, which is why he balked at any attempt to slow down the growth. Then, on the day that Goang published its latest quarterly earnings, Li sold all his shares of Goang and disappeared. Insider trading at its best. A very ingenious way to launder money, but Li probably overlooked the fact that anyone realizing unusually large gains on the stock market becomes an easy target for the authorities.

With renewed desires to completely disappear from both criminals and authorities' radars, Phil and Bianca silently, deep in their inner thoughts, head out to their apartment complex in Bali. Usually armed with ideas and new plans, Phil closes his eyes only to find the lack of any paths to a solution. At a minimum, he would like to offer words of encouragement but he knows how fake he would sound. He decides to just lean his head on the taxi's backseat's headrest to avoid having to face Bianca's interrogating look.

Chapter 22

Bianca insists that they shop for furniture in Bali, so they have at least one place to call home. Although Phil doesn't think it's safe to stay at the same location for too long, he finds comfort in Bianca wanting to settle in with him. And staying too long at Paul and Linda's place might become uncomfortable or suspicious.

The couple is in-and-out of specialized boutiques, constantly switching from tropical weather to air conditioned almost-refrigerator level temperatures, to negotiate with shop owners selling furniture. They place some orders that will take weeks to be delivered – Phil wonders whether they will ever receive the purchased items. After more than $55,000 spent on sofas, beds and tables, Phil is exhausted and pleads with Bianca to spend the rest of the afternoon in the pool.

Back to the complex, Phil receives a distressed call from Gilberto, who has been babysitting the employees of Equit and trying to coordinate the currency booths' operations around the world. Multiple problems have surfaced. Inflows from both Norrid and Li's group have completely dried out. No one is picking up phone calls in either organization. As a result, the currency booths are now only operating from legitimate business flows, which barely cover their costs. The currency conversion business probably won't survive long if it cannot pay its rent and employees. Asking for bank loans is out of the question, because lenders would want to see the details of the operation.

Without money flowing through the booths, Equit's inflows are choked off, and the crypto scheme had to be stopped. Jack Frey, the Raptor turned crypto trader, receives daily threats from Alex to start trading again. Gilberto had to put Jack on 'medical' leave to stop the harassment.

Finally, and more importantly, dirty money was being used to pay the generous benefits to Equit's employees. With no money received whatsoever from dirty sources, the upcoming rent payments on the luxury residences of the employees cannot be made. The exotic cars were paid for upfront, so at least the employees still have something to show for.

Phil tells Gilberto that he doesn't have an immediate solution and he will get back to him. Phil decides to try calling Ernesto again. Surprisingly, he picks up.

"Ernesto, where have you been? We have massive problems on our hands here," Phil exclaims.

"Look, once in a while, we all have to tighten our belts. Norrid's resources are temporarily not available. Actually, I would appreciate if you could please negotiate with Li for Norrid to exit Equit. With the performance of the last few months, our investment must be worth a fortune. I am sure Li can make Goang buy us out," demands Ernesto.

"Keep dreaming. Interpol is after our friend Li for insider trading of the Goang stock. Li is nowhere to be found and his organization has completely stopped the cash inflows into our booths. Therefore, Equit is now also in trouble," explains Phil.

"That's unfortunate. Well, I'm sure Dr. Debo and yourself can figure a way to keep things afloat at Equit until we're ready to operate Norrid sustainably again," says Ernesto in a paternalistic tone.

"Ernesto, without influx of money, we'll suffer from major desertion of staff, perhaps including yours truly," says Phil.

"Remember, I told you to never leave your family behind. This organization will eventually get back on its feet and go after any defection of its beloved children. I gotta go. Talk to you soon, and be smart," concludes Ernesto as he quickly hangs up.

Phil asks Bianca to join him in their empty apartment, so that they can call Dr. Debo together in order to strategize. They need to have a plan before Norrid's financial duress attracts attention from authorities.

"Dr. Debo, I guess your knowledge of Norrid's practices was spot on; Ernesto also warned me against leaving Norrid. And in no uncertain terms," says Phil using his mobile's speaker phone, so that Bianca can listen in. Her eyes fill up with tears as she feels that there is no possible end to this nightmare.

"Indeed, any plan for a quick escape would not be advisable. And without your involvement in managing Equit and the currency booths, it would quickly become a mess. Those businesses need to continue to operate. A failure of Equit, given Goang's involvement would become public knowledge and attract undue attention, potentially tracing back to any of us, irrespective of where we try to hide. This is not just the United States' reach anymore. Authorities from Hong Kong and Singapore would get involved," explains Dr. Debo in a very calm voice, as if he were lecturing the students of an Ivy League school.

"This is insanity. These crazy criminals have left us with a sinking ship, that we have to continue to manage, otherwise we get caught. It's like a hot potato, that

Ernesto just dropped on our lap. And if we refuse or flee, they kill us," says Phil, grabbing his hair in disbelief.

"Phil, Equit is not a sinking ship. It is now managing over $200 million of assets, generating enough income to pay for the employee benefits that we've been paying with dirty cash since the inception. The employees shouldn't even notice," says Bianca with exceptional composure.

"You're right. Goang, however, will definitely notice a large drop in profitability next quarter. I guess we have enough time to figure out the message or story to be concocted for Goang and its shareholders," concludes Phil, building from Bianca's sudden clear-headed approach.

Unfortunately, Phil and Bianca will have to go back to Singapore in a few days to orchestrate all of this. They really need to keep Equit 'business as usual', especially as far as staff perception is concerned.

For the currency conversion operations, Phil believes that it would be better to close the individual booths that cannot cover their costs relying solely on legitimate business flows. This will mean closing more than half of the booths globally. They do not see any other alternatives, so they call Gilberto to make the change.

Back to Paul and Linda's apartment for dinner, Phil and Bianca try to act as normal as possible. Although Phil had warned Bianca to avoid any drinking altogether, she agrees to sit down with Linda on the balcony for a glass of wine. She turns to Phil with a celebrating grimace, and he answers with a dirty but flirtatious look. He will probably have to intervene later to avoid any unintentional slip-ups. Phil can already hear Bianca yap about something in relation to Singapore.

Paul takes the opportunity to take Phil to his home office. He starts by showing off pictures of himself with celebrities and politicians taken at various charity events, then recounts some of his career accomplishments. When

Paul closes the door, seemingly to avoid that any part of the discussion be heard by Linda and Bianca, Phil knows that this is going to be a serious conversation.

"You know, I've been thinking about getting back to work. I feel like I need to do something productive again," says Paul, clearly looking for Phil to take him onboard in some capacity.

"That's great Paul, you should always follow your dreams. It's never too late to start on a new path," says Phil, in a completely innocent tone.

"Well, I was wondering if I could help in any way with your business, it sounds so exciting. Or perhaps we could start a new venture together. What do you say?" asks Paul, with less insinuations. He approaches Phil and taps him on the shoulder.

"Hum, I don't think that there are any immediate needs with the limited projects that we are running at the moment, but I can let you know in the future. In the meantime, if you have a genius spark for a new product, let me know, and I'd be happy to help," says Phil, thinking about how Paul has no idea in what kind of trouble he could be in by getting anywhere near Norrid.

"I can work for free as an unpaid consultant! Come on, I'm bored out of my mind here. Let me join you guys in Singapore. I'm a go-getter, I'll help you solve problems," pleads Paul.

"Let me think about it. But hey, why do you mention Singapore?" asks Phil.

"Oh, I just overheard you talk to someone on the phone earlier about some work issues and I think Bianca just mentioned something about Singapore, so I assumed that's where you're going next," replies Paul.

"Alright Paul, I'll give this some thought," concludes Phil, wondering whether Paul somehow knows more than he cares to admit.

Chapter 23

Onboard the jet, waiting for clearance to depart to Singapore, Phil decides to call Bruce, the CEO of Goang, to float the idea of Goang buying Norrid out of Equit. This may actually be an honorable way to discharge some of the problems – onto Goang. Since the harm of public disclosures through Goang's financial statements has already been done, might as well leave them with the entire quandary.

Phil quickly pitches the idea to Bruce, who starts nervously laughing. He tells Phil that the company's attention is being diverted to more pressing needs at the moment. Phil immediately imagines the worst with investigators asking all kinds of questions about Equit. Too curious to hold back his questions, Phil asks what the cause for concern is. Bruce explains that Goang just received an unsolicited offer to buy all the shares outstanding for HK$90 per share, valuing the company at more than US$1 billion. Goang has two days to answer, so he tells Phil that it's good he called, actually, it would be great if Phil could come to Hong Kong and help him and the board of directors to evaluate the situation. Phil tells Bruce that he has an urgent business matter to attend in Singapore, and he will get back to him.

Yet another layer of issues. Bianca explains to Phil that if Goang accepts the offer, there will be 'due diligence'. A special review, normally conducted by an accounting firm, which will scrutinize everything at Goang and Equit. The entirety of the companies' transactions and ledgers, from the crypto schemes to the luxurious employee benefits will have to be explained. This potential takeover of Goang has to be blocked at all cost.

Phil tells Sergio to reroute the jet to Hong Kong. A few minutes later, Sergio comes back on the intercom with the bad news that the airport in Hong Kong is extremely busy and no landing slot is available until the following morning. Phil calls Bruce to tell him that he will be there early tomorrow and to wait for him to discuss all the options.

Only in Singapore for a few hours, Phil calls a staff meeting at Equit. He thanks all the employees for the outstanding performance of the past quarter. He calls out the first-class accomplishments of the currency trading desk. Phil also lets the employees know that Ernesto and Li will be absent for a period of time, so all questions and issues should be directed to him. He gets interrupted on a few occasions by laughs and jokes cracked by arrogant traders, who believe that the success of Equit is entirely due to them and whoever is managing doesn't matter. Others also interrupt with genuine questions and concerns, especially towards Li, who has not returned any calls for a few days.

Finally, Phil asks the staff to continue their great efforts, especially now that the crypto star trader, Jack Frey, will probably not be returning due to personal reasons. Alex almost has a heart attack. He waits for Phil to finish his speech and jumps from his seat to ask Phil to meet with him for a few minutes. They enter the nearest conference room.

"What the heck Phil? What happened to Jack?" asks Alex.

"I'm not exactly sure. He has some kind of medical issue," answers Phil.

"Phil, you better find me another exceptional crypto trader, the success of Equit and our currency desk depends on it," says Alex, impatiently.

"I am very much aware. But count your blessings my friend. You and your team have personally benefited from Jack's trades, so I know exactly why you're angry. I'm not even sure that you care about Equit's viability. Anyhow, it is as much your responsibility as anyone else in this company to find a replacement for Jack. So, get to it right away, and stop whining," replies Phil, with a condescending tone borrowed directly from Alex's style.

In order to avoid more questions and complaints from the overpaid whiny and cocky employees of Equit, Phil leaves with Bianca to quickly buy proper attires for their meeting in Hong Kong. In the offices of Norrid and Equit, overwhelmingly staffed with millennials, wearing casual clothes, sometimes even flip flops, is acceptable. Meeting with the board of Goang is another level though.

After some painful and expensive shopping at a Singapore mall, they head back to the airport. Sergio has secured a landing slot in Hong Kong at seven o'clock, leaving limited sleep time, especially given the four-hour flight from Singapore, which barely qualifies as a red-eye flight. Bianca gives one of her sleeping pills to Phil and he is knocked out almost immediately.

They wake up at eight o'clock, still in the air. Phil storms into the cockpit, only to learn that Hong Kong's control tower has put them on a holding pattern due to adverse weather in the area and heavy inbound traffic. Their probable landing time is now nine o'clock. There is absolutely nothing Sergio can do to speed things up as the large commercial aircrafts seem to have priority over Phil's small jet.

Goang's board meeting starts at nine thirty. Phil and Bianca probably won't arrive at Goang's offices before ten or even eleven o'clock. Hopefully, that will give them enough time to convince the board to push back on the offer.

Without sufficient knowledge of the city, Phil and Bianca jump in a taxi upon their arrival, ignoring Bruce's advice to take the incredibly efficient train to the Central area of Hong Kong. Stuck in traffic and heavy rain, Phil calls Bruce's office multiple times but fails to reach anyone. Bruce finally sends a text message to Phil with instructions to reach Goang's board room on the 75th floor of the IFC building.

Phil and Bianca are finally let into the room at eleven o'clock. They introduce themselves as special consultants and interim managers of Equit. The board members are cordial to their visitors and delighted to finally interact with 'hero' members of Equit's team. However, Phil definitely feels the exhaustion in the room and that the board is ready to move on with a plan.

Bruce places a few documents in front of Phil, which he starts to walk through. Barely five seconds in his seat, Phil flips the pages of the offer documents and suddenly puts his hands on his forehand and starts rubbing heavily. He just found out who is offering to buy Goang's stock: KexCorp Industries.

Phil is visibly not feeling well. His whole existence is crashing in front of him. On one hand, how is it possible that KexCorp became interested in the only thing that Phil is involved with at the moment? But at the same time, how could Phil not even think that Henry's curiosity would drive him to study a company whose stock price rose so rapidly?

Although completely distracted by the turn of events, Phil listens to Bruce, who speaks non-stop for 15 minutes.

Bruce presents his team's analysis of the offer, the potential synergies with KexCorp, in other words, the expenses to be potentially saved by leveraging KexCorp's infrastructure, and the need to capitalize on Equit's previous quarter of performance, which may or may not repeat in future periods. In summary, Goang's board is ready to agree and let KexCorp's analysts and advisors review all their records, including those of Equit.

Phil listens intently to Bruce and the various board members that express their opinions, all supporting the decision to accept KexCorp's offer. Phil is incredulous as he listens to each one of them, speaking as if they were accomplished business executives, perched at the top of the city overlooking the little people on the street from the 75th floor. Goang was going nowhere before its association with Equit, but benefited excessively from criminal activities and the absolute greed of Li. Phil needs to quickly think about ways to unravel this, or, at a minimum, buy time to slow down the upcoming invasion by KexCorp. He jots down some notes and ideas as he listens to each argument, while continuing to flip through some of the documents in front of him.

It is past noon when Phil is finally invited to share his thoughts, but service employees interrupt the meeting to roll in carts of cold sandwiches and salads. Bruce suggests to break for 30 minutes. Perfect, that will give Phil some time to call Dr. Debo and huddle with Bianca before presenting his arguments against the offer.

After lunch, Phil initiates his half-prepared and half-improvised presentation to the board of Goang. He starts by warmly thanking them for the opportunity to share his thoughts and that he understands how critical this decision is for the shareholders of Goang. Then, he spends a few minutes describing the nascent operations of Equit, which as Bruce pointed out, could have had a lucky quarter that never repeats. Or, it could potentially make much more profits down the road, which would then command a higher share price than the HK$90 offered by

KexCorp. Phil reminds the board that Equit made a substantial investment of salaries and benefits to attract the best talent in the world. Once Equit reaches its full potential, the investment in talent will pay off juicy returns. And for the moment, given a special bonus paid to key employees, they cannot easily leave.

Phil also talks generally about his experience working in large multinational companies like KexCorp – without admitting that he actually worked for KexCorp. To realize the synergies of an acquisition such as the one proposed to buy out Goang, KexCorp would have to integrate the operations of Goang and Equit into their systems and infrastructure, also potentially cutting back on workforce. Phil explains that this could remove the corporate identity of Goang and Equit, and trigger the loss of confidence and motivation of personnel that are key to the success.

Finally, Phil explains that although Goang now benefits from 80% of Equit's profitability, all management decisions must be made jointly with Norrid following the true sense of the joint venture agreement. Since Norrid's confidentiality could not be guaranteed if KexCorp were to review Equit's operations, Phil believes it unlikely that Norrid would agree. Therefore, collaborating with KexCorp would be strictly limited to Goang's operations, exclusive of its of investment in Equit. Given that Equit's performance is probably the primary driver of KexCorp's interest in Goang, the collaboration sought by KexCorp might be fruitless.

As Phil scans the room, looking at each facial expression, he attempts to gauge whether he has convinced at least a majority to turn down the offer. It is still not in the bag, so Phil decides to push the envelope with a few lies based on shaky grounds.

"I have a lot of experience with transactions of this type. KexCorp is hoping to strong-arm this board with its vast amount of resources. They have set an artificial deadline of two days. Your first move should be to ignore the deadline in order to place yourself in a position of power," says Phil, trying to make the board members feel insulted by KexCorp's offer.

"But Phil, what if they decide to pull their offer back?" asks Bruce.

"It is unlikely. In fact, in most cases, that will lead them to offer even more money," replies Phil, with his most confident voice.

"If they pull back their offer, wouldn't the market assume that KexCorp found something wrong with Goang, which would negatively affect us?" asks one board member.

"Quite the opposite. It will put Goang in a position of strength, perhaps even drawing more potential suitors into the mix, and as a result, drive your share price even higher. You will essentially become like the most beautiful hard-to-get girl in the class that all boys are dying to date," concludes Phil.

The board members are impressed with Phil's delivery, and agree to provide no answer to KexCorp. They mandate Bruce to wait until the deadline has passed to call KexCorp's CEO to say that Goang will not issue a response. They also ask Phil and Bianca to stay in Hong Kong for a few days in order to support developments with KexCorp.

Chapter 24

Henry is furious. He's irritated that Goang's board is turning KexCorp down. During their brief conversation, Henry tries to strong-arm Bruce into cooperation by reminding him that he may become his boss soon. Bruce, a traditional and well-spoken British National with a strong accent, keeps his calm, which annoys Henry even more. Bruce assures Henry that he is acting on specific orders from Goang's board and its advisors.

Who do they think they are? If they want a battle, Henry is ready for war. He has crushed competition, led global transformation initiatives and convinced the most difficult world leaders to deregulate industries, so he is not about to be stopped by a small Asian company. Henry asks Josh to assemble a team of investment bankers, lawyers and accountants to prepare a revised offer for Goang.

After hours of closed-door meetings, Henry is fed up with the pessimistic advice from everyone around him. They are all squarely against pursuing an acquisition of Goang, except Henry. He feels a sort of personal vendetta. An urge to prove to the board of Goang that he is the one calling the shots. Only he gets to decide when it is time for KexCorp to make a move. People need to fall in line. Henry throws all the professionals and bankers out of the room, and asks Josh to immediately summon his public relations team.

Josh is uncomfortable because he agrees with the advisors. Going after Goang is just not worth it. There are a lot of unknowns, especially given that the activities of Equit are somewhat obscure, with only the limited public disclosures made by Goang. But Josh knows better. He knows that his boss can have a horrible temper. Arguing with him at this moment will not make him change his mind. Henry might actually dig in his heels in even more. Josh will have to wait for the right opportunity to reason with Henry.

The public relations team enters Henry's office. Josh tries to excuse himself, but Henry insists that he stays to help. Henry announces that he wants to make a hostile takeover bid for Goang, at a price of HK$100 per share. With such a move, KexCorp will make the offer directly to the shareholders of Goang, without any collaboration nor approval from Goang's board.

Josh feels like he was struck by lightning. He cannot believe that Henry would launch KexCorp down such a risky path. Despite knowing how difficult Henry can be, Josh cannot help but attempt to intervene.

"Henry, why don't we think this over until tomorrow, let the dust settle down a little," offers Josh.

"I've already thought about it enough. We need to move in before someone else does. At HK$100 per share, Goang is still cheap. This acquisition will help us consolidate our presence in Asia, and given the complimentary aspects to KexCorp's existing businesses, we will realize important synergies," says Henry, looking down to the streets of Manhattan, hands in pockets, with the authority of a Commander-in-Chief.

"Sir, we would run the risk of weakening Kexcorp with an investment of well over $1 billion, for which we haven't even secured financing. Without access to management and the careful analysis of inside information, we have no idea what we are getting ourselves into. We don't even know what their joint venture in Singapore is all about," says Josh, his hands together as if he was praying in order to plead with Henry.

"It's your job to find the information that we need to make this acquisition work. And don't talk to me about the management of Goang. They are incompetent. I don't see the value that they would contribute to this process anyway. In a few weeks, the board of directors of Goang will be replaced and every member of the management team will be on the streets, begging for a job," concludes Henry, feeling as emboldened as ever.

The public relations team is quiet, moving their heads back-and-forth as if there was a tennis match between Henry and Josh. They also cannot believe that they are about to be in the middle of a hostile takeover bid, which could bring a wave of negative publicity onto KexCorp, especially on social media, where a mischaracterization of KexCorp's intentions could erupt in a nano second, and would require massive public relations efforts to fix.

Despite the disapproving look of his Head of Public Relations, Henry orders a press release prepared first thing in the morning with information about Goang and the amount that KexCorp is about to spend. Before Josh exits the room, Henry reminds him that while his insights and hard work are appreciated, the final decision always rests with himself and himself alone. He also asks Josh to ensure that the Legal department files all the proper paperwork with the Hong Kong Stock Exchange or any other applicable securities authority in order to ensure that no laws are breached.

Henry sits in his office. As usual, he feels like the weight of the entire company rests on his shoulders. More than ever, he feels alone at the top of the world. He is confident though, that once more, this acquisition will prove hugely profitable for KexCorp, and he will again be vindicated. He knows, however, that the upcoming battle with the board of Goang will be taxing on his senior management team. It will also be a potential distraction from all of the other pressing needs, priorities and challenges that KexCorp has been facing, before the conversations about Goang even started. This battle will need all of Henry's credibility, courage and determination.

Chapter 25

Bruce and the board members of Goang have no idea what hit them when they wake up less than two days after turning down KexCorp's collaborative offer. The front page of the South China Morning Post is reporting that Goang, a home-grown company, is being targeted by an aggressive American multinational. The article hypothesizes that Goang's technology, know-how and manufacturing base in China could be leveraged for expanding distribution to the Americas and Europe. No mention of Equit or the cryptocurrency aspect.

The board will gather for an emergency meeting at ten o'clock. Bruce is desperately looking for Phil and Bianca.

The jet couldn't be parked at the Hong Kong airport, and Phil didn't want to check into a Hong Kong hotel to avoid having his passport copied. They also could not enter mainland China to potentially stay in nearby Shenzhen because they do not have Chinese visas. So, the couple had decided to fly the jet to Macau, the former Portuguese colony that is now part of Greater China. Parking in Macau is easier because the airport is accustomed to accommodate the private jets and helicopters of Asia's richest families that come to Macau for gambling and other leisurely activities.

Upon waking up at eight o'clock, Phil, who was expecting a slow day relaxing with Bianca, perhaps watching a show or roam around the casinos, notices the frantic messages from Bruce and calls him back.

"Did you see the news?" asks Bruce.

"No, what's going on?" asks Phil.

"KexCorp is launching a hostile takeover bid on Goang at HK$100 per share. We need you here for a board meeting at ten o'clock," says Bruce, in a panicked voice that is at odds with his usual slow and thoughtful British tone.

"Alright. We're in Macau. We will take the speedboat and should arrive at your office around ten thirty," answers Phil. He had already looked into how to get from Macau to the Central area of Hong Kong the fastest way possible.

Knowing Henry and his personal pride, a hostile takeover bid doesn't surprise Phil all that much. It is, however, astonishing that KexCorp would want to pursue this small company and be ready to pay so much. Given the current state of Equit, especially without the crypto scheme running like it was, Kexcorp is looking at a sizeable write-off if they complete this acquisition.

When Phil and Bianca are just minutes away from getting on the boat at the Macau ferry terminal, Phil receives a call from Ernesto.

"I need your help to untangle Norrid's finances. You need to come to Zurich, Switzerland right away." Requests Ernesto.

"Right away would be hard. I'm trying to sort out the mess that KexCorp is creating with Goang, which will further expose Norrid if we let it happen. Can you wait a few days?" asks Phil.

"No. Norrid's priorities are far more important than whatever can possibly happen to Equit and Goang. I need you here now," says Ernesto, categorically.

"Let me call you back," says Phil.

Bianca offers to go to Zurich to help Ernesto while Phil continues to deal with Goang's board. Phil knows that it is a good idea but is concerned about her security risk. Phil calls Ernesto back to say that Bianca will go now to assist him, but she will have a security guard with her at all times. And Phil will join them a day or two later.

Phil then calls Sergio to tell him that Bianca is on her way back to the plane and he needs to take her to Zurich, and that he, or Claudio, needs to be with her at ALL times, while the other is watching the plane. Also, Phil wants Sergio to text him their location every few hours and ensure that Bianca securely sleeps in the jet every night. Sergio is left with the impression that Phil is overprotective of Bianca, which doesn't seem to match Phil's otherwise self-confident nature, but he just agrees to follow whatever his boss tells him to do.

Phil finally arrives at Goang's office. This time, the board is waiting for him to start the meeting. Despite KexCorp's hostile approach, Bruce and the board members are in a surprisingly good mood. They all own shares of Goang, and the stock is up more than ten-fold from just a few short months ago. It seems to Phil like they are ready to give in to KexCorp. Therefore, Phil believes that it is absolutely necessary that he continues his fear tactics. He explains to the board that they, and probably a large number of Goang's staff, would all lose their jobs as soon as Henry takes over, especially with a hostile takeover, where mutual trust would be difficult to reestablish.

Moreover, Phil attempts to scare them with the prospects of costly lawsuits if KexCorp finds any irregularities down the road. KexCorp will use any excuse to claim that certain financial information was not properly disclosed in

Goang's financial statements. Phil doesn't go too far down that line, but he knows that the public description of Equit's operations by Goang was misleading to say the least. Lawsuits by an American corporation or investigations by authorities would drag Goang's board and management to court rooms, perhaps for the rest of their lives. They would also have to pay more money to lawyers than they would ever have made by selling their shares of Goang.

While they query Phil about the prospect of lawsuits and job losses, it becomes clear to Phil that these men are well-off and they think, perhaps incorrectly, that the payday that they would receive from the offer currently on the table would be enough to send them to retirement under the sun. They are concerned, however, about the loyal employees of Goang who could end up on the streets. Board members also worry about negative public perception. Hong Kong is a relatively small circle of tycoons and other rich people, and giving the perception that they gave in too quickly to a large American multinational firm bothers them.

Phil exploits this concern by suggesting that Goang goes on the offensive with its own public relation efforts. He suggests that Goang issues a press release immediately to make clear to investors that the board believes that KexCorp's offer is too low and undervalues the core operations of the company. Also, Phil recommends that Goang pretends that it is in discussion with other strategic partners, which will make KexCorp believe that a bidding war will ensue. Phil is thinking that this tactic might terrify Henry about overpaying for Goang, and he would just give up.

The board agrees to take this battle public and asks Bruce to bring in Goang's Head of Public Relations. However, a few members express to Phil that it is very important that KexCorp doesn't completely withdraw its offer. Bruce wonders whether there could be a sort of back channel communication with KexCorp. Phil, of course, would love that KexCorp gave up, but he is not about to admit that to the board. Instead he says that he can reach out to a high ranking official at KexCorp, whom he knows. He is thinking about Josh. Phil also suggests to look for a true 'White Knight', a company friendly to Goang that would come in, offer slightly more, and save Goang from being bought out by KexCorp. Phil proposes that this White Knight could be Norrid.

Chapter 26

Due to the sophistication of airport controls in both Hong Kong and Switzerland, Phil decides to use his proper name and passport to buy a first-class seat on a Cathay Pacific flight to Zurich. Upon boarding, he receives text messages from both Bianca and Sergio that they safely landed in Zurich. It is mid-morning in Switzerland, so they are going to head out to Norrid's office after lunch. Given Phil's flight duration and the time difference, he should be able to meet with them for dinner. Exposing Bianca to Norrid's operatives for an afternoon on her own, seems like an acceptable risk. Therefore, he is able to relax and sleep on the flight.

Ernesto is impatiently waiting for Bianca in the lobby of the Prime Tower, one of the most prestigious buildings of Zurich. Bianca wonders how long Norrid would be able to afford such luxurious rent if the organization doesn't get back on its feet quickly. She introduces Sergio to Ernesto and explains that he will remain close to her until Phil arrives. Ernesto is confused for a moment but understands the safety concerns. He seems to be distracted, and in a hurry to get to work.

Bianca is welcomed to a large conference room full of paper files, laptops, and mobile phones. Ernesto asks

Sergio to sit outside the room at a desk where he can see Bianca through a glass door but cannot hear any of the conversations.

"While the team is out for lunch, let me explain what we are trying to figure out," says Ernesto, as he points to a world map showing where all the operations of Norrid take place, heavily concentrated in Latin America and the U.S., with sporadic presence throughout Europe and Asia.

"Please try to keep this conversation to financial details only. I don't want to know how this organization generates money," interrupts Bianca, trying to immediately establish the boundaries of the discussion.

"Fair enough. See, we have two primary issues. First, our cash inflows were interrupted by a joint FBI/DEA bust into our sales operations in the U.S. They are also investigating our primary banking partner in Columbia for not having sufficient anti-money laundering controls, which has completely frozen all of our accounts there. Sales channels are being fixed and the cash collections are picking up again, but our infrastructure to channel that cash into our laundering mechanisms is broken and will take months to rebuild. We need to find a new route for the money from the street level to our legitimate businesses. Meanwhile, the cash is just sitting idle with our people all over the place, in potentially unsecured locations," explains Ernesto, trying to sound as intelligent as possible, but Bianca already knows that he is intellectually limited. Bianca gives Ernesto a blank stare with her arms crossed over her chest.

"I guess it is a financial aspect, but perhaps a little too close to the dealers. I don't want to be involved in that. Maybe Phil can look into it when he arrives. What's the second problem?" asks Bianca.

"Well, most of our legitimate businesses around the world are not exactly self-sufficient without the extra cash inflows. Some businesses are not breaking even anymore.

We need them to stay alive and be ready to receive cash in a few months, when we're all back to normal. We can't afford to lose the massive investment that we've made to build this network. Or even worse, we could attract the attention of authorities if our businesses are forced into bankruptcy proceedings by unpaid suppliers or employees," says Ernesto.

"I can look into the financials of those companies and give you some recommendations. Give me the list of all the entities, their primary activities and the Ostriches that I can contact to dig into the details," says Bianca sternly, with a long sigh that exhibits her frustration with having to get involved with Norrid's dirty mechanics. Ernesto has no possible chance to say more or disagree with her.

Phil texts with Bianca upon landing in Zurich and agrees on a restaurant to meet her and Sergio. He breezes through security and customs, and heads over to the taxi stand, which is in high demand at this time of the day. After more than 25 minutes waiting in line, he finally gets in a cab. To his surprise, a large black man in a suit gets in the same car, but on the other side.

"Excuse me. Euh, one of us just got into the wrong car. Do you mind?" says Phil, with his best condescending tone.

"I am special Agent Turner with the FBI," says the man, flashing his badge and his service weapon, low enough so that the taxi driver cannot see it.

"Pleased to meet you. I'll just get another taxi then. You can keep this one," says Phil as he opens the door. But before he is able to step out, another agent pushes him back to the middle seat and also sits in the car.

"Phil, you're coming with us for questioning," whispers Agent Turner, and he tells the taxi driver to head towards the district of Oerlikon.

The FBI agents give multiple confusing directions to the driver in order to disorient Phil. They suddenly stop in front of a warehouse. Phil hesitates between screaming and seeking help from the driver, or collaborating with the agents in order to continue to give the impression of innocence. He chooses the latter. There is really no point in having questionable behavior in front of the FBI. Acting innocent is probably the best avenue.

They enter through the side of a building and descend two levels of stairs. Agent Turner puts a dark hood over Phil's head as they go through a few doors that seem heavy and modern from the sounds they make while unlocking and opening. Phil also hears the heavy tone of electromagnetic locks as the doors close behind them. This place sounds guarded, perhaps some sort of safe house for U.S. agents operating in Switzerland. Planning an escape would need more sophistication than when Phil was initially confronted by Norrid's operatives in Jakarta and Singapore.

The agents sit Phil at a small table with his hands handcuffed in front of him. They remove the hood from his head to reveal a small interrogation room equipped with a large mirror on the wall facing Phil, most likely giving a view to other agents, observing and listening from another room.

"We're not here to hurt you. We're here to help," says Agent Turner.

"Then, why am I cuffed? You're certainly not here to arrest me if you're FBI. I'd be surprised if you had any kind of jurisdiction here in Switzerland," says Phil, clearly laying out the irregularities of the situation.

"We're investigating a crime that involves American individuals and companies. To that effect, we are collaborating with Swiss authorities," explains Agent Turner.

"The newspapers are going to love this: Held in a secret cave: American businessman arrested, cuffed and detained by the FBI in Switzerland. I have friends at the New York Times and the Washington Post, and they love to point out government screw ups," says Phil with his best poker face.

"That won't be necessary," says Agent Turner, after looking at the other agent, in a clear sign that they wouldn't want any information leaking to the press.

"Look, we all know that you're doing something illegal here. Cut the crap and set me free. I have important business to attend to. The longer you keep me here, the more it will cost you," says Phil.

"Actually, we're here in hopes to secure your cooperation. To work with us," says Agent Turner as he frees Phil's hands.

"What do you mean?" says Phil, now standing and walking around the room, rubbing the handcuff marks on his wrists.

"We have reasons to believe that Norrid is involved in a money laundering operation and secretly hides its fortune right here in Zurich. We think that you can help us find the missing pieces to this puzzle," says Agent Turner, looking deep into Phil's eyes, trying to denote any nervousness or reaction.

"Look, I help many organizations with various financial transactions. I cannot disclose the names of my clients and I certainly cannot disclose anything about their transactions. Unlike you, I follow laws and regulations, and I will comply with the Non-Disclosure Agreements that I have signed and my professional code of conduct. Unless of course a judge were to relieve me of my obligations. I would be quite surprised if a qualified judge were sitting behind this mirror," says Phil, alternating between lies and his patchy knowledge of courts and legal obligations.

"When the FBI offers collaboration with an individual, both parties benefit. I would recommend that you reconsider, especially with the evidence in our possession," says Agent Turner.

"If you had evidence against someone or a company, you would have already gotten an arrest warrant, and wouldn't be wasting your time with me in the basement of an industrial building in Zurich. My presence in this room, multiple floors underground is evidence that you are on a massive fishing expedition. Therefore, unless you want your names all over the press for harassing an American on a business trip, you need to back off now," says Phil with confidence.

"Ok, as you wish. We'll give you a ride to wherever you need to go," says Agent Turner.

"No, thank you. Just bring me back to the airport," concludes Phil.

The agents put a hood back on Phil's head and lead him to a car, then drive him back to the airport. He walks around the terminal trying to determine whether anyone is following him. He decides to avoid taking any chances venturing into the city again, so he texts Bianca and Sergio that the dinner is cancelled and to meet him back at the jet.

Chapter 27

Onboard the jet for the night, with Sergio and Claudio checked in a nearby hotel, Bianca debriefs Phil on the problems faced by Norrid. She also relates to Phil that she had to stop Ernesto in his tracks when he wanted her to get closely involved to the operations associated with consolidation of cash from street-level dealers.

Phil decides not to reveal his encounter with the FBI to Bianca because he is not sure that she can take that kind of stress at the moment.

He listens attentively as she describes what she saw on the maps and the understanding that she gained from the financial information of the thousands of legitimate businesses of Norrid. Phil comes to the realization that Norrid is a mammoth conglomerate. If the businesses around the world truly cannot survive without the laundered money and go bankrupt one after the after, it might create shockwaves through the economy of many countries, be the subject of undesired press coverage and bring scrutiny from politicians.

Phil reflects on Norrid's inability to take physical cash from the street dealers' hands to Norrid's businesses. He wonders if the dealers could become the clients, whether fake or real, of those companies, which would ensure that the legitimate businesses stay afloat. If the dealers could somehow buy products of the businesses using their cash on hand, then it would solve both sides of the equation in one transaction. However, we're talking about physical cash, and physical goods. How could they be paired up? Oh, but wait, they do not have to. Phil's got it. He knows how. He needs to talk to Ernesto.

Given the uncertainty about whether they would be followed by FBI agents going back to the city, Phil calls Ernesto and tells him to meet in the jet early tomorrow morning. Phil gives lame excuses about not having time to go in and out of Zurich, because he needs to get back to Hong Kong in short order. He also doesn't want Ernesto to know that FBI agents have approached him.

Ernesto knocks on the jet's door at six o'clock the following morning. Phil and Bianca are still asleep, their unclothed bodies glued together. Phil peeks out of the window, sighs loudly, and tells Bianca she can stay in bed while he talks to Ernesto. Phil dresses quickly, opens the door to welcome Ernesto, and asks him to join him in the cockpit, so that Bianca can sleep some more. That will also avoid that she hears the plan that Phil wants to share with Ernesto.

Phil explains to Ernesto his idea for getting money from the street operations of Norrid to the legitimate businesses:

1. The street resellers will use the money on hand to buy prepaid debit cards (issued by the global payment processing companies) at pharmacies and other retail stores across the U.S.

2. They will then take pictures of the cards' numbers and send them to a team of Raptors.

3. The Raptors will post the products of the legitimate businesses in auctions on popular websites. Then, using phony usernames and addresses, they will buy

those products themselves using the prepaid debit card numbers.

4. They won't actually ship any product. On the auction websites, the Raptors will just click that products have been shipped from the seller side and click that it's been received by the buyer. The Raptors will control both sides of the transactions. It will of course leave a commission for the websites used, but that's the price to pay to launder this money.

5. The global payment processing companies will transfer the funds to the auction websites, which will then deposit the funds into the accounts of the legitimate businesses of Norrid.

Phil explains that it's important to keep the General Managers of the legitimate businesses in the loop because funds will start showing up and the Raptors and Chameleons will need to arrange the ledgers of the companies. Also, products will be posted online, and actual customers could show up and buy the products that will need to be delivered to avoid complaints by users to the auction websites. Complaints could generate attention online through customers' reviews, and then potentially attract attention to the scheme, which could be picked up by authorities.

Once again, Ernesto is proud of Phil. He smiles and keeps nodding his head up and down.

"You've just singlehandedly saved Norrid. I don't know what I would do without you," says Ernesto, tears in his eyes and a hand on Phil's forearm, like a proud father.

"It's just a simple idea, and I'm not sure whether it will work and for how long. One of the companies involved (one of the payment processing companies or the auction websites) might wake up to the scheme and limit our abilities. Anyhow, we can test it on a small scale for a few weeks to see if it works, and then ramp up from there," cautions Phil.

"We will need to build up quickly. Some of our businesses are already going under. Please go back to Kuala Lumpur and set this all up with Gilberto. He will know how to contact the street operatives," concludes Ernesto as he gives Phil a warm hug, opens the cockpit door, and gets off the plane.

Phil joins Bianca back in bed. He cuddles with her warm and unconscious body. She wakes up, smiles, embraces Phil and slowly opens her eyes. She asks Phil why he came back to bed with his clothes on. Phil loves the insinuating question and starts kissing her intensely. He decides that he will update her later on his conversation with Ernesto and their upcoming task, waiting for them upon their arrival in Kuala Lumpur.

Two hours later, the love birds are back to sleep when Sergio and Claudio open the plane's door. They apologize profusely and start getting setup in the cockpit. Sergio lets Phil know that he has secured a landing spot at the Hong Kong airport. Still half asleep, Phil processes Sergio's statement for a few seconds. Since he hasn't heard from Bruce, he assumes there is actually no burning issue in Hong Kong, so he orders Sergio to change the plans and head towards Kuala Lumpur instead, in order to start planning for the prepaid card scheme with Gilberto. Sergio sighs and shakes his head in frustration and enters the cockpit.

As Phil is thinking about Bruce and Goang again, he suddenly remembers that he forgot to talk to Ernesto about Norrid potentially being the White Knight to buy out Goang. It would have been a waste of time anyway. Norrid's current financial state of affairs is such in a disarray, that there is no way Ernesto would even entertain such a plan. But if Norrid is in financial difficulty, Phil wonders whether Agent Turner was right in saying that Norrid had significant resources hidden in Switzerland to supposedly take advantage of the bank secrecy laws. And if that's the case, why wouldn't Norrid use those resources to save its businesses. Perhaps Norrid considers its assets in Switzerland sacred and doesn't want to open up the coffers to avoid attention from authorities in other countries. This is a high stakes mystery that Phil prefers to avoid altogether. He has enough problems as it is.

Chapter 28

Bianca is not happy with Phil's new plans for Norrid and doesn't want to be part of it. She tells him that he really needs to turn on the legal part of his brain because there has to be ways to make those legitimate businesses profitable again without continually reverting to dirty tricks. Phil promises that he will also think of honest ways to resolve this mess. They both know that Phil's words are starting to sound like empty promises, borderline lies. Bianca is annoyed. She rolls her eyes and turns away to sulk.

"Maybe I should just go back home to Australia. My parents are starting to worry about me anyway," says Bianca, still looking away from Phil.

"Baby, I promise that we're going to figure a way out of this. Now wouldn't be a good time to leave. Norrid would track you down," says Phil as he wraps his arms around Bianca.

"So, where exactly am I allowed to go, according to the Norrid's rulebook?" asks Bianca.

"To avoid raising anybody's suspicions, I think we need to stick to the same places, right here in South East Asia," says Phil in a soft voice.

"Alright then, we'll drop you off in Kuala Lumpur, and then I'll go to Bali with the jet to hang out with Linda for the week," says Bianca categorically.

Phil unsuccessfully tries to smooth out the drama but it's a lost cause. So, he asks Sergio to fly her to Bali, keep the plane there for a few days, and come back to pick him up Friday night. Phil then tells Bianca that he will meet her in Bali for the weekend. Upon disembarking, Phil blows a kiss to Bianca and asks her to follow-up on the furniture delivery and to limit her drinking sessions with Linda. She answers with a grimace.

Back to the office, Phil explains the prepaid card scheme to Gilberto and Dr. Debo. Together, they immediately start mapping out the steps of the implementation. The Raptors in Vietnam have been less busy recently because of the slowdown in the currency booths, so assigning five of them to the new scheme is easy enough.

One of the Raptors picked for this new scheme is Robert, who is actually the smartest of the group. Phil and Gilberto explain the scheme to him over the phone. He immediately gets it and agrees to start opening the phony auction accounts with various websites right away. Dr. Debo leaves to mobilize his Chameleons to setup the documents for the scheme, for example, the fake shipping manifests.

Towards the end of the day, Phil and Gilberto call Arturo, who is in charge of most of the street resellers in the U.S. Arturo had been given notice by his superior at Norrid to expect the call.

"Arturo, we need your guys to use the cash that the street operatives have on hand to buy prepaid debit cards at various merchants, then send us pictures of the numbers and destroy the cards," explains Phil.

"You expect us to show up at pharmacies with stacks of money to buy this stuff? They have security cameras in those places. Bringing bags of money in there will get us detected," says Arturo.

"Actually, you're right. The purchases have to be small and discrete. So, they need to buy other items like cigarettes or chewing gum, and then ask the cashier for a few hundred dollars of prepaid cards at the same time," says Phil.

"A few hundred dollars? My guys are sitting with hundreds of thousands of dollars each. How many pharmacies or other retail stores do you expect us to visit?" asks Arturo.

"For now, just have them buy a few hundred dollars each, and we'll let you know when to industrialize it," commands Phil, leaving Arturo limited ability to disagree.

"We can do this first batch but if you think that my guys will spend all their time driving around to visit shops for debit cards, you're dreaming. And you need to keep track of who is sending what. This thing could become a mess when we try to determine how much each dealer is supposed to have," concludes Arturo

It was the first time that Phil heard the term 'dealer' in his interactions with Norrid. He knew full well that Norrid was a drug cartel, but he definitely preferred the terms that Ernesto has been using like 'sales and collections'. And it seems like some resistance will be felt from that division. Asking them to show their faces in stores will bother them. Let's see if Ernesto will need to get involved again to make sure that the troops are cooperating.

Then, Phil and Gilberto start booking conference calls with the General Managers of the legitimate businesses. There are thousands of them, so they group them up by country on conference calls. Given the large number of participants on each call, Phil remains generic and just says that they are opening a new sales channel on auction websites to improve their profitability. When he mentions that all activities will be centrally managed by the Vietnam accounting team, all the General Managers immediately know the nature of the initiative and do not ask any questions.

Throughout the week, Phil and Bianca text frequently but do not talk over phone. It is the first time in months that they are apart for more than one day. Phil thinks that she might have needed some time away from Norrid – and himself. So, some distance might help get her energy back. However, he keeps texting her some romantic messages to get a general sense of what she is up to. Primarily to avoid that she gives in to excess drinking, which apparently makes her an open book.

Phil also texts with Paul to help keep an eye on Bianca, more for safety purposes. Paul embraces his role and gives daily updates. He is actually becoming increasingly casual and friendly with Phil, who doesn't mind but remains fairly guarded, not knowing Paul's true intentions.

Bianca spends the entire week with Linda, chatting about fashion and clothes, and judging people on the beach. Bianca learned 'people-watching and judging' from her experience on Brazil beaches and is now proudly putting it into practice. The gals actually behave on the alcohol side, limiting their consumption to a few daily margaritas. Enough to be happy and relaxed, but remain in control.

On Friday morning, Phil texts Bianca that he misses her and cannot wait to see her again. She replies reciprocally and warns him about a surprise that will be waiting for him in the jet when Sergio comes to pick him up in the afternoon and adds a 'lol'. Phil is expecting a gift of some sort or even better, Bianca in a silk night gown, waiting for him in bed. His imagination is running wild, so he decides to stop inquiring for more information.

Chapter 29

By mid-afternoon on Friday, Sergio and Claudio land the jet in Kuala Lumpur. Phil has a few hours of work ahead of him, so he tells Sergio to have Claudio rent a car to come pick him up at the office. By the time he drives to Kuala Lumpur's downtown area, Phil should be ready to go.

At five o'clock, the receptionist knocks on Phil's door to say that someone is waiting for him at the reception. Thinking that Claudio has arrived, Phil packs up his office and heads towards the entrance. In total shock, he sees Paul chatting with Tiago in the reception. Tiago, hands on his hips, frowning eyebrows, gives a dark look to Phil that means 'what is this guy doing here?'. This is certainly not the surprise from Bianca that Phil was hoping for.

"Hey Phil, happy weekend!" says Paul.

"Paul, what are you doing here?" asks Phil.

"Bianca didn't tell you? I pleaded for her to let me come to pick you up. Hey man, nice jet. Can I see your office? I'm dying to see what your workspace looks like. I miss corporate life so much," says Paul.

"Ah, I just locked everything up. Another time maybe," says Phil as he presses the elevator button. "Let's just head back to Bali."

"Actually, why don't we have a few drinks here in Kuala Lumpur before heading back. It's my first time out here, I'd love to see the city," asks Paul as he taps Phil's shoulder, like if they were old buddies from high school.

"Maybe. Tiago will take you back to the car. I just need five minutes, I'll be right with you," says Phil as he turns away. Tiago puts his arm around Paul to lead him to the elevator. Paul doesn't resist. He can feel the heavy weight and strength of Tiago.

After the elevator doors shut, Phil calls Bianca. He wants to yell at her for letting Paul know that he has a jet and worse, letting him get on it. But when Bianca picks up, she has a loving and tender voice, so Phil decides to adopt a soft approach. She admits to inadvertently letting out that they have been traveling on a private jet, but Paul had become so annoying about going to pick up Phil, she didn't know which excuse to give him anymore. Phil lets her know that he will have a drink with Paul before flying back to Bali, so he will probably arrive past midnight. Bianca answers that she will be waiting for him, unclothed in their newly arrived bed, and to make sure to wake her up when he arrives. Phil is glad that their romance seems to be unaffected by the drama caused by the introduction of the prepaid card scheme.

When he arrives in the parking garage, Phil is greeted by Rod, his personal chauffeur, whom he has not seen for weeks. Rod says that Paul and Tiago are waiting in the car and they sent Claudio back to the airport. Phil doesn't like to lose control of the situation and feels trapped, once again, by Norrid's operatives. But he goes with the flow anyway.

They drive only a few blocks and stop at the Traders Hotel to visit the SkyBar, a fancy cocktail venue with a pool occupying the majority of the surface on the top floor of the hotel. Rod stays in the car, but Tiago comes out to accompany Phil and Paul. While they are walking towards the elevator, Phil tells Tiago to stay close but not too close.

Paul seems so excited to be out. He starts chatting up various people standing by the bar, talks flirtatiously to waitresses, and orders drinks as if he were the owner of the place. That behavior, in addition to his flowery Hawaiian shirt, is drawing a lot of attention. Phil is not used to this and becomes uncomfortable. He continuously scans the area for threats or irregular sightings.

Across the pool, Phil notices a group of Asian men, visibly high rollers given the many liquor bottles on their table. Phil is staring at the group. One of the Asian men, wearing a hat and large sunglasses waves discreetly at Phil, who immediately looks away, looking for Tiago, who is now out of sight.

Phil tries to keep cool as he sits in a corner, allowing a view of the entire place. Paul comes to sit with him after a few minutes. Paul is in such a good mood. Phil doesn't want to ruin his night but is really looking forward to leave this place. The Asian man with the hat and sunglasses approaches their table. When he is just a few feet away, Phil realizes that it's Li.

"Li! Wow, I didn't recognize you. Good to see you! It's been a while, how have you been?" says Phil, giving a bit of a show in front of Paul, hoping that Li will play along to avoid tipping Paul on their murky business relationship.

"I'm good Phil. Who's your friend?" asks Li. Phil makes the introduction between the two. "Phil, let's go for a ride, I have something to run by you," says Li.

"Ah, I'm just relaxing here Li. Can we talk about it over phone tomorrow? Or even better, I will be back in the office next week," says Phil, looking around the bar to spot Tiago, and trying to make Li go away.

"It wasn't an invitation Phil. I really want you to come with me," says Li as three men approach Phil and Paul. Those three were also present in Cairns, when Phil and Bianca had the pleasure to meet Li and his thugs.

Phil doesn't want to make a scene and potentially alert authorities, so he stands up and asks Paul to come along. At this point, bringing Paul with him might be just as risky as leaving him alone at the bar. He might start calling the police and bring attention to Phil's activities in Malaysia. They walk towards the exit and into the elevator to the hotel's lobby. Still no sign of Tiago.

When the group steps outside, Phil notices Rod, standing beside his company car, looking at the scene. Phil gives Rod a deep and stern look, hoping that Rod understands that a volatile situation is unfolding, and perhaps he will think of alerting Norrid's Enforcement Division.

Li asks everyone to board a large Mercedes Sprinter van. Phil gets in first and suddenly stops as he sees Tiago lying on the floor of the vehicle, bloodied and seemingly unconscious. Phil's reflex is to check on Tiago to see if he's alive. He has a pulse and seems to be breathing. Li tells Phil and Paul to keep walking towards the back of the van. Once everyone is onboard, they start driving. Phil is fearing yet another detention.

"What have you done to Tiago? Is he okay?" asks Phil.

"He's fine. He had an accident, probably hit by a car. We are just helping him get to the hospital. He should be just fine," answers Li.

"Li, I have done everything you asked of me. Now it's your turn to hold your side of the bargain and leave us alone," says Phil, trying to remain as calm as possible.

"True, but since I sold all my shares of Goang, my organization doesn't have a channel to benefit from the booths operations anymore. Phil, I don't have a way to invest the fruits of my people's labor," explains Li.

"You must have cleared a nice amount of clean money with the sale of your Goang investment, so aren't you happy with that? Your people should feel very proud," says Phil.

"Phil, it's never enough. Resources are piling up again. I need a new way. Come work for me, I'll pay you three times what Norrid gives you. And you obviously need new and better protection. I can provide that for you," says Li, with his hands open towards Tiago body.

"Three times, Phil, you should really consider the offer," says Paul innocently. Phil turns to him, wondering if he's in cahoots with Li or just too dumb to understand what is going on.

After a 45 minutes ride, the van stops abruptly. Voices can be heard outside. Then, a soft knock on the side of the van. Li puts his index across his mouth to make sure nobody makes a noise. There are no windows in the back of the van, so it is impossible to know what is going on outside. Li pulls his cell phone and dials-up someone, presumably the driver of the van. No one picks up. He opens the door. Two policemen are standing outside the van, their hands on their holstered service weapons. The officers require that everyone get off the van.

"What's going on in here?" says one officer, in broken English, as he notices the lifeless body on the van's floor. Phil is imagining the worst: rotting in a Malaysia cell for accessory to bodily injuries sustained by Tiago, perhaps even murder if he were to succumb from whatever trauma he suffered.

"Officers, we found this man lifeless on the sidewalk. We are driving to the hospital," says Phil.

"Would you be so kind to offer a police escort?" asks Li.

"We'll take him ourselves," says the other officer.

The policemen drag Tiago's body to an unmarked squad car. Phil and Paul help fit Tiago's body in the back seat. Li and his guys take the opportunity to speed away with the van, which doesn't seem to concern the officers. They ask Phil and Paul to also get in the squad car. Phil hesitates for a moment. They are in the middle of nowhere. Should they try to escape, on foot, from these police officers? Phil doesn't even know which direction to go. Moreover, they would be fugitives in a foreign land. And, what if they pull their guns and start shooting. It's not worth it. They all squeeze in to fit in the car. They start driving fast to get Tiago some medical help. Phil and Paul's bodies get crushed on each side of the car, when the flabby and heavy mass move side-to-side, every time the car takes a sharp turn.

The officers park the car at a certain distance from the hospital entrance. The driver turns off the engine and turns towards Phil.

"We are Norrid operatives. Your chauffeur Rod alerted us of this situation. You need to go in alone and avoid questioning from anyone. Tell the hospital's triage that you are not sure how this happened and leave as soon as you can without leaving your name," says the driver.

"How am I supposed to drag 250 pounds? This is madness," asks Phil.

"We're sure you'll figure it out. We'll take your friend back to the airport. When you're at a safe distance from the hospital, call your driver to pick you up."

Phil tries different ways to hold Tiago for the 200 feet walk to the hospital emergency entrance. He decides that it'll be more efficient if he runs to the door to get someone's help or grabs a wheelchair. So, he leaves Tiago's body on the sidewalk. Once in the hospital, no wheelchair in sight, just a receptionist. He asks her to come help him to bring in an injured patient. She radios in for help and jumps from her seat to come to the rescue. Phil only then realizes that she is probably less than 100 pounds. Nobody else around at the moment, so that will have to do.

Phil grabs Tiago by his armpits and she takes his heavy feet. By the time they enter the hospital, two nurses arrive with a stretcher. They start asking Phil dozens of questions and order him to follow them. Phil tells them that he is not sure how it happened, perhaps he was hit by a car. He says he just found the body on a sidewalk in the downtown area. Phil slows down his pace to let the nurses take Tiago. However, as soon as he takes a step in the other direction, he comes face-to-face with a security guard, who asks him to come in for questioning.

The security guard takes Phil's phone and locks him in an empty room. After pacing for 15 minutes, Phil finally sits down on the floor, hoping that Norrid's lawyers will work some magic to get him out of there. Two hours later, a police officer enters the room. This time, it seems like a real officer. He takes Phil to the police station and leaves him in the interrogation room.

Four hours later, Phil is lying on the floor, exhausted and half asleep when Agent Turner, from the FBI, and Agent Dia, from Interpol, enter the room. Phil smiles nervously.

"So nice to see you both again. What is it this time, stealing of national secrets? Wait, no, it must be smuggling of nuclear warheads." says Phil, sarcastically.

"I don't know Phil; we're hoping you could tell us. You are either attracting trouble or somehow trouble finds you. It's probably a good thing for your wellbeing that we had your profile with police databases around the world, so we got notified of your apprehension. We happened to be nearby, so we're coming to save your butt from the Malaysia police. We were actually looking at some of your finest works of art in Singapore when your name popped up on our screens. What a coincidence!" Says Agent Turner.

"Awesome! FBI to the rescue! Well, thank you for saving me. Can I leave now?" asks Phil.

"Not so fast. It appears that your friend was indeed hit by something, but it doesn't quite fit the description of a car. Perhaps more like a baseball bat? I didn't know they played baseball in this part of the world. But my question really is, why would you try to overdose him with antihistamines?" asks Agent Dia.

"Look, I came out of the Sky Bar and found him bloodied and unconscious, so I took him to the hospital. You're making me sound like a criminal for being a Good Samaritan and trying to save this young man," says Phil, with his smart annoying voice.

"Fine. We'll vouch for you on that. But we really need your cooperation with our investigation of Norrid. We are ready to offer you a reduced sentence for your crimes," says Agent Turner.

"My crimes? You are so far out of line. I help my clients with perfectly legal transactions. Unless you're charging me with something, please let me go. I have been held against my will for too long already," says Phil.

The Agents can't think of any reasons to keep Phil for questioning any longer.

Chapter 30

Phil and Paul finally depart to Bali at six o'clock in the morning. Phil is annoyed with Paul, so he keeps completely silent. Half an hour into the flight, Paul cannot hold back anymore and asks Phil a succession of twelve questions about who these men were, the fake officers, and why were they after him. Phil has no intention of answering any of the questions. He lets Paul know that it would be better in the future if he just stays in Bali. And, that he should tell Linda that they were out all night, and never speak again of what he experienced.

Entering the Bali penthouse at nine o'clock in the morning was not exactly what Phil had in mind for a romantic night with Bianca. She is still asleep though, so he quietly slips under the covers. Bianca wakes up, squinting from the sun rays coming through the bedroom.

"You either had a lot of fun last night with Paul or got into some kind of trouble that I'm not too sure I want to know about," says Bianca with a smile.

"Yep, that's right," says Phil.

"Trouble?" says Bianca as she pulls herself from the pillow and scans Phil's body for any harm.

"Well, Li resurfaced and ambushed Paul and I. The Norrid guys saved us. But I don't know if Tiago will survive. We had to leave him at the hospital," explains Phil, with a deep sigh. He leaves the FBI part out of the conversation.

"What did Li want this time?" asks Bianca.

"New ways to launder his cash. The idiot sold his shares of Goang, so it is now useless for him to inject cash into Equit, as he can no longer profit from the venture," says Phil.

"Equit was the perfect setup for him, he really blew it. I think we just need to stay here for a while, it's so peaceful," says Bianca as she gently rubs Phil's back.

Phil's busy Friday didn't allow any time to catch up on news. Finally relaxing by the pool on Saturday afternoon, he turns on his phone and scans what is being reported by the main outlets. KexCorp and Goang's public relation departments issued at few statements, accusing each other of various things. Phil smiles as he now sees a reduced likelihood that the transaction would come through. He is also happy that there is now enough press, allowing him to contact Josh, by strictly referring to details available in the public.

Despite the time (middle of the night in New York), Phil takes a chance to ring Josh's cell phone, who might be hard at work because of this transaction. Sure enough, Josh immediately picks up.

"Josh, it's Phil."

"Phil, good to hear your voice. You don't sound like you're on this side of the world. And it's not like you to work long hours during the night anyway," says Josh.

"Well, I never had to because I was so productive during the day," replies Phil, continuing their friendly rivalry of the past.

"Ah, you're right, but sometimes patience and refinement produce the highest quality deliverables. Joking aside, what can I do you for?" asks Josh.

"Listen, I just read that KexCorp is going after a random Hong Kong operation. I guess you're probably involved in this, so I thought I'd call to let you know what is being said in the Asian business circles. You have to promise to not reveal that I called you to Henry, or anyone else for that matter," says Phil, sounding as if he had heartfelt concerns about KexCorp's financial situation.

"Of course, I won't reveal the source. To be honest, some of us are actively looking for ways to convince Henry out of doing this deal. He has been so stubborn, as you can imagine," reveals Josh.

"Yeah, I'm glad that I don't have to deal with this kind of stuff anymore. Alright, so apparently, there are some irregularities with the company that you guys are targeting. I don't know the full details, but some insiders are allegedly trying to make KexCorp cough up more money and are happy to head for the exits because the value is not there," explains Phil.

"Really? Wow, that's crazy. Thanks for the tip and hopefully we can all get out of this graciously. Hey what are you up to these days?" asks Josh.

"Not much. Just relaxing and getting into small consulting contracts. Really just enjoying retirement," lies Phil.

"Would you consider working for us, just for this transaction? You could really help us, especially with how Henry values your opinion," pleads Josh.

"Nah, I don't want that much stress. Thank you for the offer though, it's really nice of you. Good talk," concludes Phil.

In a better mood, feeling confident that Josh will find a way to reason Henry, Phil turns to Bianca and winks with a content smile of self-congratulation. In spite of the ups and downs of their journey, and the sporadic evil-minded solutions that Phil has concocted, Bianca is truly happy with her new life. She is proud of how Phil and her continue to beat the odds of surviving through the obstacles brought to them by powerful organizations.

Phil gazes intently at Bianca, also feeling the increasing strength of their relationship. He feels awful, however, that he is hiding important details from her. Perhaps revealing the FBI encounters would be a start. Just as Phil is about to finally sum up the courage to open up, Bianca squeezes his hand, and pulls him over for a kiss. She whispers softly that she finds him so hot and can't resist anymore. They hurry back to the penthouse. The FBI story will have to wait for another time.

Chapter 31

Monday morning comes and Phil thinks it's better to head back to Kuala Lumpur to finalize the setup of the prepaid card scheme. He decides to bring Bianca along because Phil doesn't think that being around Paul is safe anymore. Moreover, the Enforcement Division proved to be somewhat effective in Kuala Lumpur, so perhaps staying close to them will be beneficial for safety purposes.

Phil never imagined that he could bring himself to ever miss or appreciate Tiago's presence. Now, however, Phil really wishes that Tiago has recovered and is ready to get back to work. It seems like he might have really put himself in harm's way to defend Phil.

When Phil and Bianca arrive at the office in Kuala Lumpur mid-afternoon, they are surprised to see the place starting to come back to life. A dozen of employees are moving in furniture and files, and wait, even Ernesto is in his office, talking on his cell phone, clearly unhappy about something. When Phil passes by, Ernesto frowns and waves at him to join him in his office.

"Ernesto, I didn't realize that you would be back here today," says Phil innocently, wondering if he should feel bad for arriving in the office mid-afternoon, a practice that would have definitely brought disapproval from his superiors during his corporate years in New York.

"Well, since you've found another way to feed our cash, I was planning to be here later this week to re-open the office. But I got a call from Li on Saturday. He said that Tiago and you harassed him Friday night. I found this out of character for you, so I flew in earlier to find out what happened," says Ernesto, sounding like a father whose children mischiefs are causing grief to neighbors.

"Ernesto, Li completely ambushed us. We were just trying to get out of his way," Phil says as Ernesto continues to frown.

"Phil, Li is just looking for ways to partner with us. Perhaps they could participate in the currency booths again, which would help us stay afloat for the time being. And the last thing I need right now is to start a war with Li's organization. Call him and be nice. Make things happen," says Ernesto, driving shock waves into Phil's body.

Phil doesn't disagree with Ernesto's request to collaborate with Li to infuse more cash in the booths. He is floored and offended, however, by the notion that Li is trying to make it seem like Phil instigated the violent events that took place a few days ago.

Phil wants to hear Tiago's story before calling Li. Perhaps he will remember something of the moments before he was hit and drugged. It turns out that Tiago was discharged from the hospital earlier today. Phil calls him to meet in the office as soon as he can. Less than 30 minutes later, Tiago arrives at the reception, with stitches across his partially shaved skull. He is angry, cranky and it seems like he is out for revenge, walking steadily towards Ernesto's office, ready to pick an argument. Phil stops him in time.

"Tiago, stop. Let's talk before you walk in the same trap as I did." Pleads Phil.

"What do you mean?" asks Tiago.

"Li somehow convinced Ernesto that we instigated the events that happened Friday. He wants us to collaborate with Li again. It's in the best interest of both Norrid and Li's organization. I'm as frustrated as you, but I happen to agree that coming to terms with Li is better for everyone. I know you got seriously injured, we'll just have to be more careful with these guys in the future," says Phil.

"Fine. But you can't stop me from giving Li a stern warning that if he tries to pull something like this again, he will wake up one morning with deep regrets about his life's blunders, perhaps with some of his body parts on his night table, next to his bed," replies Tiago, with fire in his eyes.

"Talking to him, on the side, is fair. However, please try to keep the violence threats to a minimum. Remember that he also has tough guys working for him – just be smarter than them. Now, tell me what you remember after we went up to the Sky Bar on Friday," asks Phil.

Tiago relates that Li arrived at the bar after Phil and Paul, and went to sit with a group of Asian men that he didn't seem to know well. A few minutes later, Tiago was called downstairs because someone had activated an emergency button right outside the building. When Tiago stepped onto the street, he was hit unconscious by some kind of pole. And woke up at the hospital. Phil then fills in the missing details for Tiago including lying in the van, presumably drugged with antihistamines by Li's guys and having to drag him to the hospital.

Phil finds it interesting that someone activated an emergency button to attract Tiago outside. The only people there were Li's operatives. But wait, Rod was also there. Could he be colluding with Li? Phil asks Tiago to pay special attention to Rod and let him know of any suspicious behavior.

After a quick call to Li following Ernesto's instructions, a meeting in 'neutral territory' at the offices of Equit in Singapore is arranged for later in the week. During the phone conversation, Li acts completely innocently about the events that led to Tiago's hospitalization.

Phil is now wondering who he can trust. In the most unbelievable turn of events, Tiago might actually be someone that Phil can rely on. It seems unlikely that he would have agreed to such bodily harm, just to create some scenario. It is clear that Li and the rest of his organization are dangerous and reckless. Ernesto continues to prove that he is a simple non-confrontational manager with deep loyalty to Norrid, but could he turn against Phil? As far as Rod, did he help or leak information to Li, or was he the one that alerted Norrid's Enforcement Division to save Phil, Paul and Tiago?

Chapter 32

Following the tip from Phil, Josh spends the whole weekend with his team, putting together a thick dossier supporting the withdrawal of KexCorp's offer for Goang. The entire analysis builds on the notion that Goang has limited intellectual property to its name, its management team has incentives to exaggerate its success and have no desire to stick around for very long. As a result, the stock is over-hyped by the Cinderella story of Equit, which is not likely to repeat in future periods.

Josh feels ready and energized to stand up to Henry for once in his career. Josh wants to prove his value to KexCorp, with the fundamental analysis that his team has prepared. He wants to shrug off the feeling and reputation that he just follows Henry like a puppy. This time he will really impress Henry by standing his ground.

Despite the insistence from Henry's assistant that he is incredibly busy and booked in back-to-back meetings for the entire day, Josh persists and decides to sit and wait in front of his boss' office for as long as it takes to see him. He just sits there, drinking coffee after coffee, preparing his speech, as if he were a lawyer about to present his closing arguments to a jury.

Around lunch time, Henry comes out smiling, his jacket in hands, followed by three men in dark suits. Josh doesn't recognize the men but assumes they are bankers, given their look. He wonders for a second whether Henry decided to exclude Josh from the team handling the Goang purchase because of his resistance. Irrespective, he needs to give his pitch to Henry.

"Henry, can I see you for five minutes before you head out for lunch?" asks Josh.

"Josh, you have two minutes," replies Henry.

"Sir, we prepared this analysis to shed light on many irregularities with Goang..." says Josh, before getting interrupted by Henry.

"Josh, we're moving forward. We've already bought 30% of Goang's outstanding shares. You have been an excellent soldier for KexCorp all these years. And, if you want to continue to work for me, you will have to fall in line. You must listen carefully to my instructions. Will you be part of the team?" asks Henry.

"Of course, sir. So, you want us to carry on, irrespective of any evidence that would call into question the value of Goang?" asks Josh.

"That's correct. Unless Asia falls off the face of the earth, there is nothing whatsoever that will stop KexCorp from taking Goang. Our credibility and strength in years to come depends on it. If we were to give up now, someone else would move in, and our ability to acquire other companies in the future would be affected forever. We would be the cowards of the financial markets. Now, get on a plane to Hong Kong today, and be ready to file all the paperwork for a shareholders meeting of Goang as soon as we have accumulated enough influence, which should be within days," concludes Henry as he walks out.

Josh has never seen Henry so determined. His pride has clearly clouded his normally sound and calculated judgment. Josh feels hopeless in saving KexCorp from rushing down this horrible path. He wishes that he had all the freedoms that Phil is currently enjoying in his retirement – so he thinks. After securing his 'Do Not Invest' dossier in his office, so that he has an 'I told you so' card to use with Henry later, Josh heads home to pack his luggage for his upcoming trip to Hong Kong.

Meanwhile, Bruce is pacing the floors of Goang's offices in Hong Kong. He has been watching, in astonishment, the number of shares that KexCorp is accumulating. An increasing number of Goang's shareholders have already signed their intention to agree to the offer. So, he decides to call Phil for an update on the prospects of Norrid coming in as a White Knight.

Phil pretends that he is still trying to chat the executives of Norrid about the prospect of investing in Goang, but in reality, he sees no chance of this happening given Norrid's current financial disarray. He is surprised, however, to hear that KexCorp has already accumulated 30% of the shares. They will soon control Goang. Phil cannot believe Henry's stubbornness.

After they hang up, Phil remembers Agent Turner's claim that Norrid is holding a fortune in a Swiss bank, presumably kept away from the eyes of the authorities. While he doesn't think Norrid would spend over $1 billion on Goang, perhaps they wouldn't mind temporarily buying enough of the stock to block KexCorp from taking control of Goang. Maybe slowing down KexCorp will give Henry second thoughts. Phil decides to call Ernesto.

"Phil, have you handled the situation with Li?" asks Ernesto.

"Not yet, but we're meeting in Equit's office in Singapore later this week," replies Phil.

"Good, I'll go with you. It'll be good to breathe in the energy of Equit's staff again. I love these guys," says Ernesto, like a proud papa.

"Ernesto, I wanted to run something by you. I'm still working on trying to block KexCorp from buying Goang..." says Phil but gets interrupted by Ernesto.

"I don't know why you worry about this so much. Whatever happens, we'll just continue to pay them dividends for their share of Equit. Why do we even care who ultimately owns Goang? There's no harm there," says Ernesto, in very simple terms.

"Ernesto, American public companies, especially large multinationals must meet the highest standards of anti-money laundering rules. Any connection with the way that money is making its way into Equit could shine an unbelievably bright light on all of us," explains Phil.

"You worry too much. They would have to unravel many layers, including the currency booth and crypto schemes in order to follow the money coming from the other divisions of Norrid. All of this across many countries that are not necessarily friendly with the U.S.," says Ernesto.

"Perhaps. But it would also connect an American company to Norrid. I am no expert in the latest way that American authorities treat Swiss bank secrecy laws, but why take the chance of exposing whatever Norrid is doing or hiding in Switzerland, and as a result remove part or all of the secrecy?" asks Phil, followed by a long pause. Phil thinks that he really got Ernesto thinking. He seems frozen.

"Phil... you may have a point. How can we block KexCorp in their bid to takeover Goang?" asks Ernesto.

"We need Norrid to make an offer for Goang or buy enough stocks to stop KexCorp from having voting control," explains Phil.

"How much would that cost?" Asks Ernesto.

"Half a billion dollars, maybe more. Clean money only. It has to transit through brokerage accounts and reach the Hong Kong Stock Exchange's settlement systems," answers Phil.

"Let me get back to you," concludes Ernesto.

Within a few hours, Ernesto calls Phil back and provides access codes for a Swiss brokerage account in the name of a numbered company controlled by Norrid. He tells Phil that he can use the $100 million in that account to buy Goang shares, but has to keep it very low profile, so that Norrid's name doesn't appear anywhere in the press. This means that not even Goang can be made aware.

Chapter 33

Goang's shareholders seem to be hoping that another buyer will show up to create a bidding war with KexCorp. The stock is hovering between HK$101 and HK$105 as shareholders are clearly not completely convinced to give in to KexCorp's offer. To remain under the radar and not immediately putting upward pressure on the stock, Phil makes a few purchases every day amounting to less than $2 million per day.

On Thursday, Phil hopes that Ernesto has forgotten about the meeting with Li. He wants to avoid Ernesto participating in the meeting so Phil can control the flow, and not engage Norrid in further exposure to Li's seemingly reckless organization. Phil is planning to make it look like he is heading out to lunch with Bianca, and heads straight to the jet.

They get in Phil's car and he tells Rod to drive to the airport. Rod says that, per company policy, it is now required to have a member of the Enforcement Division in Norrid's cars at all times, so they have to wait. After ten minutes, Tiago shows up with Ernesto. Phil grumbles a low rumbling sound, irritated to have to babysit Ernesto, who's probably going to create even more issues for Phil to solve.

"Are you heading to Singapore now? Did you forget about me?" asks Ernesto, with a smile.

"No, I thought you had your own transportation. Were you planning to get on my jet? I'll need to charge you for that," says Phil, in a joking tone. It is now clear to Phil, that Ernesto is tagging along.

"Yeah, if you don't mind," says Ernesto as he gets into the car. "Your comment about charging me though, is reminding me that we need to discuss how we will pay your salary, now that we have limited cash currency on hand. We may need to put you on the payroll of one of our companies."

"Never mind, I can wait until you have cash. If you unblocked my accounts, however, it would be very appreciated," says Phil, thinking that there is no way that he would ever agree to be formally paid as an employee of these organizations, which would leave an indelible mark that would never disappear.

"We can look into your precious accounts. Tiago, please give him back his cards when you have a moment," orders Ernesto. Phil is overjoyed but hides his excitement. Access to his funds might bring freedom one step closer.

"I will need a week or two to retrieve the briefcase from one of our secure locations," replies Tiago.

Upon arrival in Singapore, they decide to head over to Equit's office, to use the corporate apartments for the night. The office is empty except for Alex's team of six, including one seemingly new member. The five veterans appear to be arguing or giving a hard time to a new recruit, named Harry. Phil approaches, in an attempt to help resolve the conflict that is brewing. Ernesto and Bianca stay back to watch Phil's diplomacy from across the floor.

Alex explains to Phil that Li brought in Harry a few days ago as the new crypto trader, supposedly an expert of that world, to replace Jack. Alex, who never actually bothered to learn anything about cryptos while Jack was there, is now finding it quite difficult to supervise Harry. And actually, it turns out that although Harry has already been trading for a few days, no documentation is matching the gains realized, so the earnings of the desk are a mess.

Phil is in total shock. Li brought in Harry as a new trader, who is not a Raptor, and who clearly is not producing the kind of clean documentation that the Chameleons were producing for Jack. What on earth?

"Where is Li now?" asks Phil.

"I don't know. He left about an hour ago," says Alex.

"Ok, you guys all go home, and we're going to look into this mess tomorrow," says Phil as he waves them off their seats.

After they leave, Phil explains the situation to Bianca, and asks her to check the ledgers to see if someone has put cash into Equit's accounts to match against the supposed fake crypto trades. While she logs into a computer and starts scanning records, Ernesto turns to Phil to inquire about what's going on.

"We'll know in a minute," says Phil, staring at Bianca's screen for a few long minutes. Suddenly, she points to a cash entry of $1 million.

"These idiots deposited cash in Equit's bank account." Bianca says in total shock. Phil has never seen her with such an angry face.

"Cash, as in dollar bills?" asks Ernesto, always one step behind.

"Yep. The bank must have made the depositor fill out a form. Nobody is supposed to be able to deposit cash for more than $10,000," explains Phil.

"We need to know how they did it. Somebody's anti-money laundering alarm must have lit up like a Christmas tree," says Bianca.

Phil calls Li, who says that he is actually staying in one of the corporate apartments on the floor below. So, they head down to meet him. Ernesto warns Phil, Bianca and Tiago to keep their anger in check, and instead collaborate to find a solution. He doesn't want any confrontation with Li's organization.

They walk into the corporate apartment that Li invaded without notice. Tiago and Li's three security personnel team stay by the door, looking at each other. Tiago, his hands on his hips, is towering over the three others, with his muscle mass probably heavier than all of them together. The events from a week ago, which have left Tiago with a bad taste in his mouth, along with many bruises, would take time to heal in the best of relationships. After all, these organizations compete, perhaps not in this part of the world, on the streets as part of highly dangerous activities. The desired cooperation by the bosses doesn't sit well with all the operatives.

Li has made a mess in the room in just the few hours that he has been in it. There are papers and clothes everywhere and large black nylon bags, which Phil easily recognizes, obviously containing more dirty cash than should be in the offices of a presumed clean corporation like Equit.

Phil and Bianca greet Li from a few feet distance, but Ernesto, trying to appear as conciliatory as possible, gives a warm hug to Li. The two spend a few minutes catching up after not having seen each other in a few months. Then, Li shuts the door, and they all sit down around a table. The security detail remains outside the room.

"Li, would you mind explaining why $1 million in cash was deposited in Equit's account and you brought in a new crypto trader?" asks Ernesto in a more direct style than what Phil is accustomed to.

"Well, as you can see around this room, I am in dire needs of clean cash, so I just thought I'd bring in some candies for the employees. You know, make them happy to finally generate crypto trades and then cut myself a check for 'security services' rendered to Equit's management," explains Li, sounding like a man who has never laundered money in his life, trying to impress a crowd.

"That's not at all how the crypto scheme works. Clean money has to come into Equit, not cash. We used to pass the cash through the currency booths first. And careful documentation has to be produced. Our guys from the currency desk couldn't make heads or tails from whatever Harry was trying to do," says Phil, in apparent frustration with what Li is trying to pull.

"I'm sure you guys can fix it and cut me my check. I really need it now. Tomorrow morning at the latest," pleads Li.

"Not everything is fixable Li. Who deposited the cash and what source was disclosed to the bank? Anything above $10,000 needs a declaration," says Bianca in a somber voice.

"We just wrote that we sold exotic cars of former employees to a dealership that insisted on being paid in cash. Norrid owns the fleet of employee cars, so that's plausible, right?" asks Li, hoping for a quick approval of his actions.

"The cars were paid for with dirty cash. They don't appear anywhere in Norrid's ledgers. There is a good chance that we are already under investigation because of this cash deposit. Let me see what I can do. Perhaps we can reverse the deposit and pull the cash back out," says Phil as he starts standing up, before getting yelled at by Li.

"SIT DOWN. I need my $1 million security service payment right now," shouts Li. His voice carries across the walls, and his security guards barge in, and approach Phil. Tiago follows Li's thugs closely and also enters the room.

"Don't even think about it," says Tiago as he grabs one of Li's guards by the back of his shirt collar, pulls back hard and holds him by the neck, a foot above the ground with just one hand, ready to take care of the others with his other hand.

"Stand down Tiago," commands Ernesto. "Let him go." Tiago throws the men a foot away and he falls hard on his side, nearly splitting his skull open on the corner of the desk. Ernesto turns back to Li. "There has to be a way to work together," says Ernesto in a soft voice.

"What if we used our currency booths to clean a few millions for you, we keep a commission of say 20%, and we pay you the rest in security services?" asks Phil followed by an approving nod from Ernesto.

"Why just a few million? Can't you handle the full $30 million that I have in this room? That would leave you with a cool $6 million in commissions. I know you need it these days," asks Li, looking like he is a drug addict hoping to get high.

"Yes, we'll take care of it. Just leave it here," agrees Ernesto. Phil has a disapproving look. He knows it will take time to clean such a large amount and some of it might have to be shipped to other countries.

"Li, can we count on you to never meddle in Equit's affairs again? We want to keep this company clean," asks Phil.

"Promised. In fact, I will leave right now and never come back. I'll send someone to pick up my checks. No less than one million per week, please," says Li.

Phil knows that there is no way to launder one million per week, especially with the whole $30 million of cash sitting in Singapore. Li either has a thriving business in Singapore or was stupid enough to bring it all here. In any case, Phil remains silent so that Li and his gang can leave as soon as possible.

Tiago walks them to the underground parking and collects their Equit access badges before they get on Li's car. Tiago is waiting for them to drive off, and is stoic and emotionless like if he were a Queen's Guard. A split second before the car starts moving, one of Li's security guard flips the bird like an immature teenager, prompting Tiago to punch through the car's passenger window. The driver stops the car again. Li has broken glass all over his lap. He looks at Tiago and says: "You will come to regret this act of senseless violence, young man."

Chapter 34

As much as Phil hates having to deal with Li's cash, and having to coordinate so many Raptors and members of the Enforcement Division around the region to transport it, the 20% commission kept by Norrid is a welcomed reprieve for some of the legitimate businesses. Phil and Bianca actually spread the money around to all the businesses in need, not just the currency booths.

While they cannot quite launder the full $1 million per week that Li had hoped for, Phil scrapes every bank account of Norrid to give Li as much as possible, even sometimes having to borrow from the prepaid card scheme until new batches of cash could be absorbed. Also, the Raptors and the Chameleons remain cautious about the sudden volume that could attract undue attention, so Li receives $800,000 at most every week. This prompts threatening calls from Li to Phil when the lower than expected amounts of 'security' checks are received by Li. Phil constantly has to remind him of the risks involved, and that he's doing his best.

Phil is also busy monitoring Goang's share price, which has been ticking up given the daily purchases that he's making. The stock is now trading at HK$110. Given that level, shareholders are no longer giving in to KexCorp's offer.

Josh, who has been camping out in Hong Kong for a few weeks, has filed all the necessary paperwork for a shareholders' meeting, but is mostly bored out of his mind, waiting for instructions from Henry, who is not even returning his calls. Out of frustration and desperation, Josh decides to call Henry's cell phone during New York time lunch hour (middle of the night in Hong Kong). Every executive of KexCorp knows that calling Henry on his cell phone is a major faux pas, unless of course there is an emergency, which is exactly why Henry picks up immediately.

"Sir, sorry to disturb your lunch," says Josh in a soft voice.

"What is the issue, Josh?" asks Henry, in a stern and annoyed voice.

"As you know, our ownership of Goang still stands at 30% with limited support from other shareholders. The stock price is moving up with the increasing rumors of a White Knight getting ready to make an offer. If we go ahead with the shareholder meeting, we might get crushed," says Josh.

"The shareholder meeting is still two weeks away, so I don't know what your emergency is. Anyhow, since you called, which means you don't have anything better to do, I'll give you some assignments. Produce a review of how much we could increase our offer to secure additional shares, but more importantly, initiate a proxy fight ahead of the shareholder's meeting," orders Henry.

"Sir, the management of Goang..." starts Josh, but Henry has already hung up.

A proxy fight involves reaching out to other shareholders to secure their vote ahead of a meeting. By obtaining their proxies, KexCorp would have the procuration, or 'power of attorney', to vote shares that it doesn't currently own, as it pleases during the shareholders meeting.

This is a tall order, and Josh feels exhausted, just thinking about how this could be done. Why would other shareholders agree to give proxies to KexCorp? They would need to be convinced that whatever actions KexCorp wants to take by replacing the board will be good for them in the long run. Josh can't even think of one argument that would convince someone to relinquish their proxy.

Josh's heart rate is elevated. He can't sleep. He tosses and turns in his bed until six o'clock. He decides that enough time was wasted and starts pacing the silent hallways of the hotel. Taking advantage one of the perks from staying in a suite at Hong Kong's Island Shangri-La Hotel, Josh has been using the executive lounge as his pseudo-office. This morning though, he is just sitting there, staring at the Victoria Harbour and the land stretching towards Mainland China, covered with buildings for as far as the eye can see.

Looking at the busy waterway, filled with commercial ships, yachts and occasional but famous junk boats with their unusual red sails, Josh's mind wanders to the early times of the British colony. The opium wars, and the succession of historical events that happened in this part of the world have led Southern China to be such an important gateway for global growth. Josh realizes that this area has really played a major role in the world's development. Although it has not seen military battles since the Second World War, it continues to be central in many modern conflicts and rivalries.

Josh wonders whether Henry's relentless drive to have KexCorp buy Goang has something to do with his American pride to take a part in the East vs West rivalry. Perhaps Henry imagines himself on the cover of the Time magazine, with a catchy title referring to him as some sort of savior that can stand up against China, especially that the takeover of Goang has turned hostile. Given his philanthropic involvement in New York City and his reputation for being the most ethical businessman around, it would even make sense that he now wants a potential Asian victory to springboard himself into the U.S. Presidential race. Josh can imagine the political campaign tag lines that Henry could use, leveraging his business and political acumen. Given Henry's relatively young age, he could even afford a stint as mayor or senator before going for the ultimate prize. Josh is amazed at his own intuition – Henry must have a hidden agenda.

Potentially using KexCorp's corporate resources to launch a political career, however, makes Josh's stomach turn. He feels like KexCorp's shareholders are really going to pay a stiff price for Henry's ambitions. If Goang is as risky as Phil made it sound, an unpleasant outcome may ensue for KexCorp and Henry – and derail any of his potential political plans. Josh feels emboldened again to attempt to stop the transaction. Perhaps Phil could help.

"Phil it's Josh."

"Good to hear from you, Josh. Is Henry finally having second thoughts about his Goang investment?" asks Phil.

"No, unfortunately. Now, he even wants a proxy fight to be able to replace the board," reveals Josh.

"Oh my... sorry that you have to deal with all this," says Phil, covering his terror at the prospect of this new turn of events. Winning a proxy war could obviously speed up KexCorp's ability to control Goang.

"Hey, could you think of any way in which someone could interfere to slow Henry down in his tracks?" asks Josh.

"Well, it seems like Henry has persisted through Goang's board's defiance, the price increase, and seemingly anything you've warned him about. I don't see anything other than a regulator or Government intervention at this point," says Phil, implying that a representative of the Hong Kong Government could cast doubt about whether a buyout of Goang by a foreign company would even be permitted, which in turn would scare KexCorp and other investors away.

"Do you know anyone in Hong Kong that could do something like that? Or just maybe say something that would give enough doubts to Henry?" asks Josh.

"I don't know anyone personally, but I know someone who may have this kind of connection with senior Government positions," says Phil, thinking of Dr. Debo.

"Excellent. If you could make the call, it'd be great," says Josh in desperation.

"Of course, I can do this for an old friend," says Phil, as he is actually thinking about his own interests rather than helping Josh.

Chapter 35

A long conversation with Dr. Debo reduces Phil's enthusiasm about the potential effectiveness of a senior Government official intervention in the KexCorp vs. Goang battle. While Dr. Debo is happy to make a call to one of his many contacts in Hong Kong, he thinks that several obstacles will prevent the effectiveness of this strategy.

First, based on Goang board's motivation and conviction to sell the company, any casual call by a senior official to Bruce would reveal minimal resistance from Goang. It is truly just Phil that was able to hold them back from selling, and perhaps stir up their desire to put up a fight for publicity sakes in order to look like they are not giving in easily. Now that the fight has been going on for weeks, they are likely to be ready to hand in the keys to KexCorp and leave with their money.

Second, if public comments were made by a senior official to discourage KexCorp, Goang's stock price would immediately reduce, as investors would head for the exits. Within hours, a lot of shareholders would turn in their agreement to sell to KexCorp, giving them a quick voting majority. If the government became convinced to block the transaction, which would be an uphill battle given Hong Kong's lightly regulated environment, only then would KexCorp be impacted. But in the meantime, they could control the company.

Dr. Debo leaves it completely up to Phil to decide the course of action, knowing these risks. Phil agrees that any action that could potentially precipitate investors to sell to KexCorp would be counter-productive. But what if the Hong Kong Stock Exchange could be convinced to put a trading halt on Goang's stock as soon as the senior Government official makes an announcement on the stock? The halt would freeze all transactions on the stock, leaving KexCorp unable to buy the additional shares needed to control the company.

Phil suggests to go as far as bribing a Government official or a Hong Kong Stock Exchange executive to motivate their cooperation with the strategy. Dr. Debo is not comfortable with that. He has maintained a solid reputation over the years by upholding the utmost professionalism with everyone outside of Norrid, and he is not ready to jeopardize that by offering a bribe.

Meanwhile, Goang's stock has further increased, now trading at HK$115, equally driven by Phil's purchases for Norrid's account and fresh rumors that Equit is performing well. This time however, it seems like the vast majority of Equit's quarterly profits will be from true performance from the managers and traders, who after all, are some of the best in the industry. Phil continues to buy Goang shares on a daily basis for Norrid's account, but for much reduced amounts. Norrid now owns slightly over 4% of Goang.

As Phil reflects on the next steps of this corporate battle, he sees no other avenue than getting ready for the proxy fight to compete with Kexcorp. In other words, Phil will need to convince Bruce and the board of Goang to go on the offensive and obtaining enough proxies to fight off KexCorp. So, he calls Bruce to say that he will be in Hong Kong tomorrow to assess the situation with the board.

Bianca, who had been begging Phil for days to head back to Bali, is not happy to hear that she will have to accompany Phil to Hong Kong. He has to promise her that they will head to Macau instead, and she can relax there, enjoy the casinos and maybe see a show, while he goes to Hong Kong to meet Goang's board. She smiles for a moment, thinking of spending the day at a luxury hotel's spa and visiting Macau. She is also relieved for not having to meet these overrated men in their ivory tower in Hong Kong. But Phil reminds her that Tiago will have to be on the jet with them, and probably follow her around in Macau. Bianca's smile turns into a displeased grimace raising one eyebrow to express a non-verbal 'really?'. She gives Phil a thumb down and he smiles lightly, and as they turn towards the exit, they come face-to-face with Alex.

"Are you two leaving?" asks Alex.

"Is that okay with you, chief? I didn't know that I needed your permission," says Phil sarcastically and starts walking away.

"Well, the staff is growing nervous about this whole battle between KexCorp and Goang," explains Alex with one hand on Phil's shoulder and visibly more mellow than usual. His self-confidence clearly affected by his team's concerns.

"You guys are doing great, you don't need to worry about this," says Bianca, with a flirtatious smile, while rubbing Alex's forearm with her hand to cheer him up.

"I think you should sit down with the team's top managers before you leave. That might help them get back to trading," proposes Alex.

Phil wouldn't want to do the kind of town hall-style meeting, that had brought so many interruptions and general whining last time. But a meeting with the top managers should be more civilized. Phil and Bianca decide to drag Ernesto into the meeting. Since he happens to be in town, and he likes Equit's staff so much, perhaps he can help to smooth everything out.

Alex and the other ten team managers take 20 minutes to explain how the news and various rumors surrounding Goang are affecting the staff negatively. In general, the concerns center around the uncertainty of how they would be treated under KexCorp, which has the reputation of cutting costs drastically and integrating operations of acquired companies into its massive bureaucracy.

Ernesto uses comforting words to pacify the group, expressing that he will not let them down or give up on the thriving start-up culture that the teams have implemented. Also, he looks towards Phil and Bianca for validation as he talks about how Norrid values its investment, and how the terms of the joint venture agreement would not allow Goang, its acquirer or successor to singlehandedly make changes. He concludes his monologue by saying that, in a way, the fact that Equit has equal shareholders with perhaps different objectives, guarantees that significant changes would be hard to come by.

Out of respect for Ernesto, especially given his paternalistic style, the Equit managers do not argue with his claims, but they are not impressed, especially that Goang earns 80% of Equit's profits, probably giving them the upper hand in negotiations with Norrid, despite the equal management rights of the joint venture agreement.

Knowing that Phil and Bianca, given their management experience with complex companies, may have more influence on KexCorp's course of action, they all turn towards Phil, with Alex taking the lead.

"Since we all know how much Equit means to Goang's profitability, we have a few proposals that would avoid massive staff defections, should KexCorp's offer go through," says Alex.

"Staff defections? Almost everyone's housing and expensive car is paid for, and you are all under generous contracts, which would require reimbursement of the welcome bonuses," replies Phil, irritated by Alex's gutsy statement, and trying to stop him down whatever path he is trying to take.

"Let them explain," insists Ernesto, in a pacifying voice.

"We know that we are under contracts, but we were thinking of negotiating a management buyout with Norrid and Goang, before KexCorp is able to complete the acquisition of Goang," proposes Alex. A management buyout implies that a group of employees would buy the shares of Equit from its shareholders, typically by borrowing money for the purchase price from a bank or other lenders. Phil sports a faint smile after hearing this, because this could actually be enough to scare off KexCorp permanently, even though the likelihood of either shareholder agreeing to this is minimal. It just needs to be a possibility working itself through Henry's mind.

"Let us give this some thought," says Phil, before Ernesto opens his mouth with another insufficiently thought-out statement. "But in the meantime, I think we would all agree that stopping or, at a minimum, slowing KexCorp down in its tracks is crucial. So, if any of you or your staff happen to own shares of Goang, we will reach out to you soon to obtain your proxy votes," says Phil, as he slowly and politely stands to end the meeting.

The potential management buyout of Equit is actually what needs to leak out. Phil's mind moves off from the government official intervention and stock trading halt to this new opportunity. He asks Dr. Debo to prepare material to be sent to the local Singapore newspapers to spread the rumor of this new twist in the battle of KexCorp and Goang.

Chapter 36

The jet touches down in Macau at six o'clock in the morning. Bianca is still asleep when Phil is ready to head out to the ferry terminal that will take him to Central Hong Kong. He gives Bianca a kiss on the forehead. She growls softly and turns the other way. Tiago is sleeping a few meters away, his oversized body cramped in a bucket seat. Phil leaves a note for Bianca to enjoy her stay in Macau but to remain close to Tiago at all times.

The ferry terminal is quiet. Phil is sweating in his uncomfortable suit. He wonders how Hong Kong and Macau, two former European colonies so close to each other, both unbelievably humid and hot, each at the doorstep of Mainland China, yet ended up with such different, almost opposite purposes. One being mostly about serious business transactions and the other one about entertainment. He hypothesizes that perhaps one really needs the other to balance out and survive.

Shortly thereafter, Phil arrives at Goang on time for the board meeting at nine o'clock. After a few pleasantries with Bruce and the board members, Phil sits down and looks at the agenda of the meeting. He notices that at eleven o'clock, the board will welcome a special guest to discuss the upcoming shareholders meeting: Josh from KexCorp.

Phil stands up again to chat discreetly with Bruce in the corner of the room. Phil stresses to Bruce the importance that his presence and general involvement in this transaction remains absolutely confidential, especially in the eyes of KexCorp. Bruce sees no issues with that and reassures Phil that he will notify the board members.

The meeting is now ready to kickoff. After going through legal platitudes regarding Goang's circumstances with the Hong Kong Stock Exchange, the board members turn to Phil for his assessment of the situation.

Phil starts by offering his view that the increase in Goang's share price is probably due to other potential suitors buying up some shares, or rumors that a White Knight and other parties would come in, driving speculative investors to build a position. This should make KexCorp reassess its offer.

As Phil expected, the board members become unhappy at the prospect that KexCorp would walk away, potentially taking a lot of value away from their personal finances. They are thinking about their personal interest instead of those of Goang. Phil takes the opportunity to argue that any KexCorp proposal would be detrimental to Goang's long term value.

"The employees of Equit are very worried about the prospects of a takeover by KexCorp. We risk general dissatisfaction or maybe even massive resignations. Either way, Equit's business model is solely dependent on highly performing employees and their know-how, so the value of the company would reduce significantly if some of them were to walk away," explains Phil.

"Aren't they locked up in management contracts?" asks Bruce.

"Yes, but that doesn't mean that they would remain motivated. And contracts are relatively short term. A minimum of interaction with KexCorp's advisors during a presumptive due diligence review would be sufficient to reveal this likely outcome. Moreover, I am in the obligation to disclose to you that the most senior employees are organizing themselves to prepare a management buyout offer," says Phil. The board members sigh loudly. They are floored by the turn of events.

"They would need to put a large amount of money on the table. Is this really feasible in such short time period? And why would we and Norrid agree to this?" asks one board member.

"They claim to have already lined up funding with a Singapore tycoon, and are ready to make their offer known to the public. This would force you to evaluate the offer for its best merits, in line with your duties to the shareholders of Goang, who could see this as a great way for Goang to obtain a large amount of capital that could be used to refocus the company on its core activities, or pay it as a dividend. And as far as I know, Norrid's officials have been in contact with some employees of Equit and appear to support the initiative," lies Phil, as heads move left and right across the room, in total surprise and disbelief, followed by a long silence.

Phil wants to take advantage of the moment to crystallize the rejection of KexCorp's offer, or, at a minimum, buy some more time. Therefore, he recommends to the board to wage a proxy fight to block KexCorp's attempt to replace the board at the upcoming shareholders meeting. Unless KexCorp revises its offer to a higher amount and is able to take control of Goang, this strategy would delay any imminent decision, allowing Goang to continue to look for a White Knight and evaluate the upcoming management buyout offer of Equit, argues Phil.

The board members had entered the room licking their chops, thinking about the amounts that they were about to cash in from the sale to KexCorp or a White Knight that they thought Phil was going to find for them. Their emotions have now soured. Phil's words calling for a proxy fight are hanging in the air. The prospects of a prolonged public relations discord and having to work with thousands of shareholders to secure their support is too much for these old men with crushed hopes of a peaceful retirement.

Trying to avoid any possible contact with Josh or any other official from KexCorp coming in to meet the board, Phil, who had constantly looked at his watch during the meeting, really needs to leave now. He tells everyone that he has another business matter to attend to. As he packs up his briefcase, he reminds the board to avoid any disclosure to KexCorp's representatives, especially as it relates to discussions with Equit, Norrid and himself. Phil swallows as he leaves the room. If they don't keep his name out of this, he could get uncomfortably called out by Josh or Henry for helping Goang, or worse, depicted to authorities as having a conflict of interest. With the FBI and Interpol already sniffing around Phil's life, this could be a catalyst for sending Phil to jail for a very long time.

Chapter 37

Despite being annoyingly flanked by Tiago, Bianca is enjoying her day in Macau. She spends a few hours walking around the touristic areas, which include rich Portuguese heritage, especially the ruins of St. Paul Church. The humidity is brutal, and Tiago is sweating profusely. Bianca feels like he needs a break, so they sit down at an indoor café for a cold drink and take advantage of the air conditioning.

After a few minutes of meaningless chatting with Tiago, he reveals that until a few years ago, he was part of the U.S. Navy SEAL Team Six, the elite group of soldiers that handles rescues and dangerous missions.

"Oh, I thought you were Brazilian," says Bianca.

"I am, but I grew up in the U.S. and became a citizen as a teenager," reveals Tiago.

"And how did you end up enrolling as a soldier?" asks Bianca.

"I've always performed better under strict discipline," says Tiago without offering more details, while continuing to scan the surroundings for any threat.

Bianca now knows why she never really had any interest in having a conversation with him: the man is trained to be quiet and deadly efficient. Bianca is really more the social and happy type – unlike the average accountant, and very much unlike a soldier.

Without unnecessarily alerting Bianca, Tiago is tracking two men in suits moving around the touristic square in front of the café. They look completely out of place from other people, especially with their suits in this unsupportable heat and humidity. They seem to be trying to escape detection but in fact are fairly clumsy and much less experienced than Tiago at undercover operations. Tiago is evaluating all options. He dials up Sergio to confirm whether any unusual activity has taken place around the jet. There wasn't, according to Sergio. Tiago asks him to be ready to depart at a moment's notice – which implies that they'll have to come back later to pick up Phil. Sergio doesn't seem ready to go along with the plan but nevertheless agrees to prepare for departure.

The quick conversation with Sergio, however, is enough to alert Bianca that something out of the ordinary is happening.

"What's going on? Should we leave this place?" asks Bianca.

"Not yet. We need to first determine who we are up against, and how many men they have following us. I can see two threatening individuals so far," answers Tiago, cold blooded as usual.

"Are there any Norrid reinforcements available in the area?" asks Bianca, almost knowing the answer.

"Nope, Norrid only has limited operations and casino investments in Macau. No boots on the ground, so to speak," explains Tiago.

After a few more minutes, Tiago leaves money on the table for the drinks and asks Bianca to slowly stand up and walk towards a back street. He sees that the agents immediately react, which confirms his suspicions. Tiago follows Bianca as he keeps scanning the surroundings to evaluate their options.

They start walking at a faster pace to reach one the main arteries. Tiago is looking around to locate a suitable mode of transportation. All he finds for the moment is a taxi, on which they get on very quickly. An old man is driving. Tiago gives him stern directions to head to the airport as quickly as possible. The driver is uncooperative and seemingly unwilling to drive fast. Tiago becomes frustrated, so he pulls up a small handgun and asks the driver to get out of the car.

Now in the driver's seat, Tiago tells Bianca to lie down on the back seat in case shots were fired. He doesn't see the men anymore, so he starts driving slowly to blend in with the traffic and avoid alerting anyone. Too late... the taxi driver, now on foot, has alerted a police officer on a motorcycle, who is now making his way towards the stolen taxi. Tiago steps hard on the gas pedal and starts weaving through traffic and orders Bianca to call Sergio and tell him that they will be at the jet in ten minutes, and that they must take off as soon as they arrive.

Three police officers on motorcycles are now in pursuit. Tiago is fairly confident that he can escape officers whose level of training pales to his. But he is no longer sure whether the men in suits are still chasing. And if they are, Tiago doesn't know if they have backup operatives and resources that can show up at any time. Finally, his knowledge of the city is not good enough to drive in alleys or places that would give him an escape advantage over whoever is chasing them. His only recourse are signs everywhere around the city indicating the way to the airport.

From the main Macau peninsula, they take the bridge to Cotai, the island that houses the airport and includes a massive area of reclaimed land where more casinos and hotels were built in the early 2000s. Tiago knows that they can't take this car chase all the way to the jet, otherwise they would be arrested way before the plane took off. They need to stop somewhere and make their way quietly to the airport. Perhaps getting into another car would allow that.

Tiago decides to turn onto the Cotai strip, a road only a few miles long with casinos, hotels and other entertainment venues on each side, similar, in some ways, to the Vegas strip. Before the police officers on motorcycles even have time to turn onto the strip, Tiago makes a quick right turn into the entrance of the Venetian Casino and stops in front of the valet parking attendant. They get off the car, give the keys to the attendant, who's clearly confused about why a taxi driver would want to valet park, and enter the casino.

Walking around the massive complex in relative normality to avoid catching anyone's attention, Tiago and Bianca slow down their pace and stop in the middle of a busy slot machine area. They sit and pretend to play while Tiago discreetly scans the surroundings. Bianca is freaking out, but she knows that she needs to keep it together in order to escape unscathed. She takes a few minutes to text Phil, who is just coming out of the board meeting in Hong Kong. He obviously gets very worried when he reads Bianca's recount of the past 20 minutes. She tells him to hurry back to the jet so that they can escape together as soon as possible.

After ten minutes of pretending to play on a slot machine, Tiago and Bianca are on the run again. They stop at one of the complex's apparel shops to buy a few pieces of clothing that will help to blend in and will make them harder to be recognized by both the police and whoever else is after them. At six foot four, Tiago's large body is hard to miss though, especially since the average size of

Asians' body frames is already less than their westerns' counterparts.

They are able to confirm with the store attendant that a shuttle bus runs regularly between the casino and the airport, so they won't have to return to the stolen taxi nor steal another car. After a few minutes waiting on the street curb, during which Tiago and Bianca feel overly exposed to every passing vehicle, they finally board the shuttle. Bianca is still exchanging texts with Phil, who is now on the speed boat from Hong Kong to Macau. They should arrive at the Macau airport at approximately the same time.

When the shuttle arrives at the airport, a dozen police officers are waiting. One of them is signaling the bus driver towards a separate area.

"Bianca, let's move to the back of the bus. How much money do you have with you?" asks Tiago.

"Approximately $15,000," replies Bianca as she hands the stack of money to him.

Tiago takes $5,000 from the stack and offers it to a man in exchange for his extra-large size luggage. The man accepts immediately. As other passengers are getting off the bus and are all facing towards the front, Tiago opens the luggage, empties it, and hides the content under the last seat. Then he asks Bianca to get into the luggage, zips it up, rolls it to the front of the bus, and asks the driver to help him to take it down to the curb.

As soon as Tiago steps out of the bus, he is swarmed by the police officers. He resists slightly to create a diversion, so that none of them think of the heavy piece of luggage left on the curb. After they've successfully handcuffed Tiago, two of the officers race inside the shuttle and come back out a few seconds later. Bianca unzips the luggage a bit, enough to witness the officers take Tiago away. Everyone around, including the bus driver, is captivated by the arrest, giving Bianca a five seconds window to come out of the luggage and walk away.

Chapter 38

Bianca holds her emotions together until she reaches the jet, where Phil is waiting for her. Then, she lets it all out in a nervous breakdown with tears and screams. Phil asks Sergio and Claudio to go into the cockpit to give them some privacy.

Phil tries to comfort Bianca as much as he can, but he needs more information before he decides whether they should take-off now or try to save Tiago. After he gets more details from Bianca, Phil calls Ernesto and explains what happened.

"This is awful, but at least Bianca is with you and Tiago is in better hands in police custody than whoever these men in suits were. I need to make a few phone calls to send a bribe to the police department. Don't leave yet, you might need to deliver some money," says Ernesto.

"Do you think the men in suits could be working for Li?" asks Phil.

"I don't see why Li would want to go after Bianca or Tiago at this juncture. Have you been paying the $1 million per week that we agreed?" asks Ernesto.

"More like in the $700,000 to $800,000," answers Phil.

"Phil, what were you thinking? He must be furious with us. Has he been following up with you?" asks Ernesto.

"Yes, and I keep reminding him that his expectations are too high. I've even scraped every penny of liquidity that Norrid has in the region to give him as much as possible," says Phil, trying to defend the huge efforts that he's been through with the Raptors.

"Phil, you should have told me. Li's guys must have been following you. How much do we owe him to catch up?" asks Ernesto.

"Approximately $1.5 million," answers Phil.

"Okay. Transfer funds to him from the Norrid brokerage account that I provided to you, and have the Chameleons doctor up some documentation to send to our office in Switzerland. Something like legal or advisory fees," orders Ernesto before he hangs up.

After only ten minutes, Ernesto calls back. It turns out that Li paid a bribe to the police to get Tiago. He is now holding him, well drugged up, in the basement of the Wynn Palace casino. Li now wants more than just the payments due. He wants an additional $500,000 of clean money, which Ernesto authorizes Phil to pay, also from the brokerage account. And Li had the guts to ask for one more thing: to get Tiago back, Phil and Bianca have to join him for a blackjack game at the Wynn Palace high roller $50,000 minimum bet per hand table.

Ernesto tells Phil to pass by Norrid's office in downtown Macau. The general manager of Norrid's operations based there can provide some Wynn betting chips.

Phil strongly pushes back on the notion of bringing Bianca back into the foray. Why take such a risk? He can go alone. And how is Li able to make all the decisions and Norrid always has to bend over backwards? And how ridiculous is it to have to play cards with Li? But Ernesto insists. A conflict with Li is not worth it. Staying in public places will be safe.

After regaining her calm, Bianca is surprisingly in favor of helping. She feels like Tiago went the extra mile for her, and after noticing the metal detectors and heavy security of the Venetian casino, she feels confident that being inside the Wynn Palace is safe. So, they get on a taxi towards Norrid's Macau office.

The office is located in the Finance and IT Center of Macau, a modern office building in a trendy neighborhood. Phil sees a pattern in the location and appearance of Norrid's offices: beautiful layout of rich wood and marble. It certainly would give second thoughts to any law enforcement agency suspecting that criminal activities are taking place. Phil and Bianca are first requested to wait in the reception area, and ten minutes later are asked to follow an assistant to the office of the general manager. They pass by an area that looks like a command center with large screens listing companies and amounts. Dozens of employees are busy pointing at the screens and typing various instructions. Bianca doesn't remember seeing a reference to this place when she was looking at Norrid's operations in Switzerland.

Francisco, Norrid's general manager for Macau, lets Phil and Bianca in his sumptuous office and offers refreshments.

"No thank you, we're in a bit of a rush," says Phil.

"Of course, the Wynn chips will be here in a few minutes. It is really nice to finally meet you. Ernesto always raves about you two. You've really made a positive impact on the success of Norrid, especially with the currency booths, that was an amazing feat," says Francisco.

"Thank you for your nice words. May I ask what kind of operation is going on here?" asks Phil.

"Sure. We offer last resort conversion services to Macau visitors," answer Francisco.

"I'm sorry, I'm not following what you mean," says Phil, puzzled by Francisco's explanation.

"Well, some organizations do not have means to launder their money or need funds quicker than what is possible to work through the casinos, so we do it for them," explains Francisco.

"Why is this last resort?" asks Bianca.

"Oh, we charge a 50% fee. So, our clients must really be desperate to use our services," says Francisco.

"And what happens to the cash?" asks Phil.

"The cash makes its way to the high-end shops in the hotels and casinos of the city through various schemes sponsored by the landlords. Our agents spend the money in whichever shop may be struggling, under performing, or just designated as needing more revenues, and bring the items back here for reselling around the world, typically through Hong Kong, on auction websites or other online stores. By spending the money in the flagship stores around the city, the shops can stay afloat, and landlords can collect their rent or even better, increase the amount of rent they charge due to increased activity in the stores. We collect commissions for our services, so everyone is happy. Plus, the sale of products helps Norrid's bottom line. Finally, the landlords let Norrid participate in all new real estate developments in Macau at a discount. So, we own participations in dozens of developments around the city that are paying us very nice dividends. Everybody wins in Macau, really!" says Francisco with a broad smile, trying some humor, with a reference to Macau's predominant industry. Bianca, never impressed with deceitful schemes irrespective of how ingenious they could be, isn't laughing. She sighs loudly, shakes her head and crosses her arms over her chest in a clear sign of protest. Francisco senses the rising tension and turns to Phil for a look of approval.

"Very interesting. Are there organizations that are more prominently using your services as opposed to setup their own laundering operations? So, you end up just being their outsourced money launderer," asks Phil.

"Only one of our clients operates like that, and represents at least a third of our business, so we charge a lower commission. It's a gentleman that goes by the name of Li," says Francisco.

Phil and Bianca look at each other in stupefaction. It is now so very clear why Ernesto wouldn't want to upset Li. He is an important client of Norrid, and he is perhaps keeping Norrid's operations in Macau afloat during these difficult times.

As they make their way out of Norrid's Macau office, Phil continues to be bothered by the revelation that Li and Norrid are economically linked. He feels like he is missing a piece of this puzzle. When Equit was created, it had appeared to Phil that Ernesto didn't know Li. Maybe that was just what Ernesto wanted to have transpired. Some form of posturing to mislead Phil. But to what end?

In front of Phil, Ernesto often looks simple and incapable of engineering the structures that Norrid needs to operate. Could this be part of his cover? Could Ernesto be one of Norrid's masterminds while giving the impression of lack of sophistication? For what purpose? Phil is not sure that he wants to know the answers to those questions.

Chapter 39

Armed with $500,000 of Wynn Palace chips, enough for just ten hands at the high roller table where Phil and Bianca are going to meet with Li, they jump in a taxi. Phil is still in the suit that he wore for his meeting in Hong Kong earlier this morning, and Bianca is sporting stiletto high heels and a beautiful white backless dress with a split on one side revealing skin all the way to her hips. Phil made her wear this outfit to distract Li and his security guards in case the situation takes a wrong turn. He made sure, however, to pack running shoes in a duffle bag for both of them in case they need to run for their lives.

They finally arrive at Li's blackjack table where he is sitting on his own, chatting with the dealer.

"I'm glad that I didn't hold my breath waiting for you guys!" Announces Li as he stands to welcome his guests, sporting a wide and fake smile, when Phil and Bianca approach the table.

"Good to see you Li," says Bianca, with an ugly grimace, as she proceeds towards Li to offer a warm hug. Then, she moves her hand down his body, slowly grabs his testicles and squeezes hard. Li reacts slightly to the tight grip prompting one of his security guards to attempt to rescue his family jewels. But Li waives him off to show that his manhood is unaffected by a woman who seems so inoffensive. Bianca puts her other hand around Li's neck and brings her mouth next to his ear to whisper a stern warning. "But next time you want to talk to me, be the man that you are. Pick up the phone and call me. No more of this bull crap with your security guards chasing me around," says Bianca, and she slowly releases her grip.

"Strong personality. Even stronger hands. I like that," says Li, in a higher pitch voice than usual, as he coughs a little and shakes his belt to relieve his genitals. Phil smiles while truly enjoying to see how Bianca is handling her 20 seconds of revenge.

"Well, threats can sometimes come from unexpected places. And people," says Phil as he pulls a chair for Bianca.

"Ya, well, don't push your luck too much," says Li with limited confidence.

The three of them sit at the table. Phil pulls out some chips and shares with Bianca, who doesn't look like she will be enjoying the game. She just stares at Li with the eye of the tiger.

"I'm glad you guys are joining me for this game. You know, we never had a chance to have a proper talk. Would you like something to drink?" asks Li as he waives to get the attention of a waiter.

"Li, where is Tiago?" asks Bianca, with a piercing look, and a tight fist on the table, continuing with her confidence.

"Who? The big dummy that you were hanging with today? I'm just doing you a big favor. The both of you, actually. Phil, you don't want that guy to hang out with lovely Bianca," says Li as he prepares his stacks of chips for the game.

"Li, we've agreed to be here as long as you release Tiago back to us," says Phil, as calmly as he can, eager to get on with the mission of retrieving Tiago and leave.

"Well, the truth is, both him AND you needed to be taught a lesson. I have been insulted too many times by your little tricks and Tiago's childish attitude," says Li, raising his voice and tapping his index finger on the table.

"You're all caught up on your clean money now, so yes, lessons learned. From now on, you will receive your $1 million installment every week until we're through with your money. But I'm curious, why wouldn't you use Norrid's services right here in Macau instead of transporting the $30 million to Singapore?" asks Phil.

"Ah Phil... You're a good money launderer, but you have no idea of the risks involved in generating and transporting money. Macau is good for Greater China. Singapore, on the other hand, is good for entry points like Malaysia and Thailand. Sometimes even the Philippines. And Singapore itself is one of our best markets," explains Li, earning a puzzling look from the card dealer. "But, sorry to bore you with all these details. I was really hoping to spend a lovely evening in the company of a beautiful woman," says Li with a flirtatious smile in Bianca's direction.

"Thank you for the compliment. I'm sure you know, however, that I'm already taken," says Bianca, somewhat disgusted with Li's advances. She looks away and shakes her head in disbelief that Li is turning the situation into some ugly form of courtship.

"Of course, I would never go behind Phil's back. Actually, I really wanted to express my feelings to you, right here in front of Phil," says Li looking straight at Bianca. "I can offer you the wealth and protection that any women would dream of," continues Li with a wide smile, exposing his stained and crooked teeth, which makes Bianca roll her eyes and look towards Phil, her palms facing upward, needing him to intervene.

"Right... So, let's get back to business, shall we?" asks Phil, in an attempt to refocus the conversation while not angering Li.

"As you wish. How much would you be willing to gamble on Tiago's life?" asks Li, which makes the dealer stop shuffling the cards and look towards the security cameras.

"This is really unnecessary, Li. Let' just..." Phil gets interrupted by Li.

"I insist. Let's put an equal amount of money on the table and play the minimum bet until each one of us gets washed up by the house. The last person standing gets to decide Tiago's fate. What do you think?" asks Li.

"How could we be sure that you will release him to us if we win?" asks Phil, liking that Bianca and he would start with two thirds of the odds.

Li signals his men to bring out Tiago. A few seconds later, two men come out of a service door, holding, on each side, the heavy and partially numb body of Tiago, and sit him down at the blackjack table. He is cut and bruised in multiple places of his face but is still faintly moving his neck and eyes. Phil shakes his head in disapproval of whatever Li has put Tiago through, and offers to start the game with each player having $200,000 on the table, so a minimum of four hands per person.

Li has a blackjack with his first hand, so he is up to $275,000, while both Phil and Bianca bust. The dealer wins the following two hands. Phil and Bianca are down to their last bet. In the next hand, Phil busts again, Bianca finishes with 18, Li with 17, and the dealer busts.

"I think Bianca and I should finish this game in my suite, what do you say?" says Li, like an old pervert.

"Based on our earlier encounter, we all know that you don't have the necessary tools for whatever game you're thinking about," says Bianca with the arrogance of a teenager. Li is humiliated and not smiling anymore. His manhood clearly affected by Bianca's comment. Phil is proud that she is able to find subtle hurtful words in this tense situation, but he also wants to complete the mission and leave relatively unscathed, so he places one hand on Bianca's thigh to make sure that she doesn't push the insults too far.

While the dealer is shuffling the cards, Phil notices some unusual activities in the distance and stands to gain a better view. Some pushing and shoving, perhaps a fight. Li perks up and becomes curious about what is going on. Suddenly, his security guards all reach for their radio, and grab Li. They quickly disappear. Bianca attends to Tiago, who is now a bit more awake. Phil grabs the chips left on the table, throws them in the duffle bag, and hands Bianca her running shoes.

Police officers arrive at the blackjack table, just as Tiago is being lifted with his arms around the shoulders of Phil and Bianca.

"Sir, what happened here?" asks one officer.

"Oh, he is just completely drunk. He passed out earlier and hit his head. We're just taking him back to his room," says Phil.

"Do you know the person who was playing at your table?" asks the officer.

"Nope, we just met him. Everything ok?" asks Phil.

"Did he indicate where he was going?" asks the officer.

"I'm afraid not. He just stood up and left. Perhaps he's at the bathroom," offers Phil to try to look as innocent as possible, so that the officers can be on their way.

Phil and Bianca painfully drag Tiago to the nearest exit, jump into a taxi and head to the airport. Phil gives an update to Ernesto and asks him to intervene again with Li, so that the unfinished blackjack game remains that way and no more meetings are necessary.

They take off from Macau. Bianca insists that they head to Bali, potentially away from Li's operatives since he didn't mention Indonesia when describing his entry points into Singapore. Tiago starts regaining his senses during the four-hour flight.

Chapter 40

Phil wakes up early morning when he hears Tiago on the phone in the other bedroom. He is ordering some form of reinforcement and equipment. Three hours later, a van arrives at the complex with metal boxes that two men roll into Phil's penthouse.

"Hey Tiago, I hope you're feeling better. You can stay with us here until you're fully recovered. We'll probably have to go back to Kuala Lumpur in a few days, so we'll just take you with us," says Phil.

"Thanks, but that's not up to you. Or me for that matter," answers Tiago.

"Alright. What is all this equipment about?" asks Phil.

"These clowns have embarrassed us enough. If they come close to Bianca or yourself again, they'll deeply regret it," explains Tiago.

"Yeah look, I'm glad that you're getting us some extra security, but we need to keep it low profile, okay? And I don't like guns and ammunitions too close to me," says Phil. Tiago raises his eyebrows and shakes his head, in a clear sign that he is not about to take instructions from Phil.

"You have no idea what it takes to protect people in our organization. Just focus on your job, and I'll focus on mine," says Tiago as he turns the other way.

Phil heads down to the pool with his computer. He catches up on the latest news and is happy to see that Singapore newspapers are finally talking about Equit's management team wanting to present a buyout offer to its shareholders in the wake of KexCorp's hostile takeover bid of Goang. The article presents Equit as a prominent, up and coming fund manager, and an employer of choice for local Singaporeans. It includes a few quotes from Alex, referencing strong and continued performance by the fund. Phil is quite happy that there is no reference to Norrid.

Back in Hong Kong, Josh, who also sees the news as he sits down for breakfast, smiles when he reads about this development. This could be what he needed to make Henry give up. At a minimum, it's worth a try. But before he even has a chance to order a coffee, Henry is already calling, obviously furious about the prospects of Equit being sold to its management. He blames Josh for letting this happen and not organizing the shareholders' meeting quickly enough. Henry hangs up the call with a loud New York style "FIX IT".

Josh is feeling stressed out. While he would like KexCorp's acquisition to fail, he doesn't want to completely alienate his relationship with Henry. So, he contacts the law firm that KexCorp uses in Hong Kong and instructs them to bring forward the plans for the shareholders' meeting. KexCorp already owns enough shares to dictate that the meeting takes place. To satisfy Henry, taking control of the board is now an absolute priority. It has to be done before Equit's management buyout is even officially brought to Goang's board.

After some back-and-forth with Goang's legal department, the shareholders' meeting is scheduled for a week from today. Bruce calls Phil to share this information.

"I'm surprised that KexCorp even wants to carry on with this, given the news about a potential management buyout of Equit," says Phil.

"Me too. But as you know, the board doesn't intend to resist KexCorp very much. Some of the mutual funds that together own approximately 40% of Goang, however, intend to vote against KexCorp's board nominations. They believe that KexCorp should increase its offer," says Bruce.

"Good. How many proxies was KexCorp able to obtain?" asks Phil.

"About 13% of the votes. With their ownership temporarily capped at 30% per Hong Kong's securities rules, they now control 43% of the vote," explains Bruce.

"Alright, it's going to be tight. I'll try to secure some proxies from Equit employees, maybe that'll give us a few percent," says Phil.

When Phil calls Alex, he is startled by the press coverage related to the possible management buyout. Alex obviously had no idea that Dr. Debo was going to leak it out with a carefully crafted anonymous letter to the press. Alex finds it interesting that the article makes it sound like the preparations for a buyout offer are more advanced than they really are. Who would even talk to a newspaper about financing details when Equit's management hasn't even approached a single lender yet? Alex is asking a lot of questions that are starting to sound like accusations. So, Phil abruptly changes topic and asks Alex for his help to obtain proxy votes from any Equit employee that happens to be shareholder of Goang. In order to make Alex have the slightest interest in helping out, Phil has to remind him that it is in his best interest to block KexCorp's push to take over the board of Goang.

Before hanging up, Alex tells Phil that the bank has called repeatedly over the last few days about a $1 million deposit. Alex says that he just told them that Phil or Bianca would return their call as soon as they are back in the office, but it has become an annoyance, so he wants Phil to call them back now.

This is not good. Li's reckless actions are having serious consequences. A Singapore bank is now associating a large cash deposit with the names of Phil and Bianca.

Phil confers with Bianca. Is it better to talk to the bank and make up a story? Or let the bank continue to investigate without returning the calls? Bianca believes that it would be best to call the bank to attempt a diversion; to tell the bank's representatives that a deposit seems to have been made to Equit's account by error, and that it probably belongs to another client of the bank.

Bianca's call is transferred through the bank's phone system multiple times before she can finally talk to the operations' manager. He seems to believe Bianca's story and says that he will put a 'hold' on the amount, essentially removing it from Equit's accounts for investigation, and refer the case to a special team that may call Bianca back if necessary. He even thanks Bianca for the honesty of reporting that the $1 million doesn't belong to Equit.

Phil and Bianca hope that the matter is behind them. Without proper rest over the last few days, they both fall asleep on lounge chairs by the pool. An hour later, Paul and Linda arrive by the pool and wake up the couple with their loud "Hello love birds! Welcome back to paradise!" greeting.

"It's been a while, how have you guys been?" asks Paul.

"Very busy, business has been non-stop," answers Phil, eyes closed, barely awake.

"Hey, we just rented a yacht for a few days, do you guys want to come along?" asks Paul.

"Sorry, we're not here for long, we have to head back in a few days, so we just wanted to relax by the pool. But thanks for the invite. Did you hire a captain for the yacht?" asks Phil.

"Oh no, I'm a sailor. I've sailed through the Caribbean islands in all kinds of bad weather, so the Bali sea is a walk in the park for me," says Paul.

"Very nice. A man of many talents," says Bianca, somewhat sarcastically. But Phil takes a few moments to digest this.

"Hey Paul, I bought a secondhand yacht recently, and I have no idea of its condition. It's in the Bahamas. Would you go there for me to check out the condition and make sure everything is in order to perhaps one day, sail it around the world?" asks Phil with a wide smile.

"Of course, I'd be very happy to help. Flip me the details and we'll head out there next week. We love the Bahamas," says Paul.

The notion of finding a qualified sailor for the yacht had been on Phil's mind for a while. Although Paul could be a bit erratic at times, Phil and Bianca might have found people they can trust to help them escape to the sea at the right moment.

Chapter 41

It doesn't take long for the $1 million deposit issue to make its way to the FBI. Agent Turner calls Phil only two days after Bianca discussed the matter with the bank.

"Phil, there is starting to be a lot of thorny questions about transactions connected to Norrid, which seem to all be pointing back to your involvement," says Agent Turner.

"Transactions? Look, I really cannot reveal anything to you due to confidentiality. I think I explained that already. But if you have a question for me, I would consider to get legal advice to determine whether I could provide an answer," says Phil, trying to indirectly bring up that the FBI would need to deal with Phil's lawyer, potentially limiting their ability to interrogate Phil or Bianca.

"I have many questions and at this point, lawyer or not, we are going to need some answers. But let's start with a $1 million cash deposit into Equit's bank account. Which part of Equit's operations would generate revenues in cash that would need to be deposited in a bank account?" asks Agent Turner.

"I understand that the bank believes that money belongs to another one of their customers, and somehow was incorrectly tagged to Equit's account. But you would really need to discuss this with the bank or Equit's management, not me," answers Phil, further twisting the story, making it sound like the bank actually believes that the money doesn't belong to Equit.

"That's interesting because the deposit documentation clearly states that Equit sold exotic cars for cash. Several of Equit's employees drive high-end company cars, isn't that correct Phil?" asks Agent Turner.

"Look, I am not part of Equit's management, I haven't driven a car in months, and I am certainly not Equit's cash manager. You're asking the wrong person," says Phil, categorically wanting to draw a line between himself and the official managers of Equit.

"Oh, I understand, should we talk to Bianca instead? It seems like she was involved in many aspects of setting up the accounting operations and systems," says Agent Turner.

"You're becoming annoying. What do you want from us?" asks Phil angrily. He wants no part of this coming back to Bianca.

"I want collaboration. I want your and Bianca's help to make my way through Equit, Norrid and any other company connected to criminal organizations," says Agent Turner, followed by a five seconds silence on the line.

"I'm a consultant and my hourly rate is very high. Are you sure that the U.S. government is ready and willing to pay such a hefty price for this?" asks Phil, with a touch a misplaced humor.

"Very high price indeed: a reduced sentence for you and Bianca," says Agent Turner.

"Here you go again with your accusations. This conversation is over. I can't wait to relate all of this to my journalist buddies. Let's see how quick your world travel budget gets cut and your butt is brought back onto U.S. soil permanently. Maybe that's what it takes to stop all this harassment," threatens Phil as he hangs up.

Phil knows that the FBI is on to something. It's a question of time before they find hard evidence that will link back to him or Bianca. They might even be trying to get other people to collaborate. What if the likes of Gilberto or Tiago started to open up to authorities? Could they bring evidence to the FBI? Could they set traps or record Phil or Bianca when crimes are being discussed? Phil is definitely starting to feel like collaborating would place him in the driver seat. Perhaps he could set some conditions for collaborating with the FBI. Does Phil possess enough information about Norrid to be sufficiently valuable for the authorities though? He only knows part of the money movement operation. He has been kept away from all the other aspects of Norrid.

One thing is for sure, Phil has to retrieve his special briefcase full of bank cards. Whatever happens to Norrid, the briefcase cannot make its way to the FBI's collection of evidence, else it would link him back to his years of corporate fraud.

On the flight to Kuala Lumpur, Phil tries to chat with Tiago as if he were an old friend. Upon landing, Phil casually asks Tiago to get his briefcase and meet back at the office. Tiago gives him the evil eye and tells Phil that if he wants the briefcase, they have to drive to a safe house together. He is not about to let him out of his sight. Phil is actually curious to find out the location of the safe house, so he agrees to the plan.

After more than an hour drive, they turn into the driveway of a large suburban house with a security gate. Two guards approach and search the car extensively, including the undercarriage. Phil's chauffeur, Rod, is clearly familiar with the procedure, he must have been here before. They then drive into an underground parking with more guards, this time armed with heavy artillery. Tiago gets out of the car and hugs with a few men who tell him that they are glad that he's alive. The stories of Tiago's captures by Li's men in Kuala Lumpur and Macau must have been discussed in the Enforcement Division ranks.

Interested to see the inside of the building and hoping to check his briefcase's content away from Bianca's prying eye, Phil gets off the car and walks behind Tiago.

"Where do you think you're going?" asks Tiago.

"I thought we had to stay together at all times," says Phil.

"This place is not for bureaucrats. Get back in the car. I'll return in five minutes," says Tiago, with his hands on his hips, looking down on Phil.

As the door leading inside the house opens and closes, Phil notices a series of automatic weapons hanging on the wall. Tiago emerges less than a minute later with the briefcase. As expected, Bianca asks what is so important about that portfolio case. Phil explains to Bianca that Norrid operatives had taken his personal effects to secure his cooperation. While she is eager to know what would be so important, Bianca continues to want to stay away from details that would associate her with crimes. She wants plausible deniability, so she just lets it go.

Back to Norrid's office in Kuala Lumpur, Phil, Bianca and Dr. Debo meet to discuss the proxy vote situation. Armed with Goang's latest shareholders registry obtained from Bruce, they go down the list to assess how this battle could play out and establish who could be friendly to Norrid to help push back against KexCorp's motion to replace the board. The current voting power percentages stand as follows:

- KexCorp: 46%
- Norrid: 5%

- Prominent mutual funds: 42%
- Equit employees: 1%
- Other diffused shareholders: 6%

The mutual funds are already against KexCorp, so no worries there. The key is to ensure that half or more of the diffused shareholders can be convinced to give up their proxy votes, which would ensure that KexCorp's proposal for new Goang board members gets rejected.

Dr. Debo starts going down the list and identifies dozens of well-known names of the Hong Kong and Singapore business communities. He knows most of them well enough to place calls in order to ask for a favor to help Goang push back against an American predator. With only three days left before the shareholders meeting, Dr. Debo agrees to start working his network immediately.

Phil sends the list of Equit employees that are shareholders of Goang to Alex for him to obtain the consent of each of them by stressing the importance that Equit can remain more independent if KexCorp is safely kept at bay. Alex agrees to help but tells Phil that what he and the other employees of Equit really want, is a management buyout. They want to be completely independent. Phil, with his best fake soothing voice, comforts Alex that everyone at Norrid and Goang understand Equit's employees' desires and want to find a mutually acceptable arrangement. This seems good enough for Alex for the moment.

Unsure of the logistics of who will vote the shares held by Norrid or any other proxies to be received, Phil calls Ernesto to discuss the arrangements for Goang's shareholders meeting.

"Ernesto, will you attend the meeting in person in Hong Kong?" asks Phil.

"Definitely not. We will need to cast the votes electronically. I'll have the Legal Team handle that," says

Ernesto.

"That would be perfect. I'll make sure that any proxies that we receive make their way to them as well. Please ensure they don't give the voting power to anyone at Goang, not even Bruce. Although he seems against KexCorp's takeover, you never know if he could be directed to act in a certain way by some of the board members who can't wait to give in to KexCorp. I don't think Bruce can be trusted," says Phil.

"That is noted Phil. Perhaps you should be in Zurich for the next few days to handle this with the Legal Team, so that no mistakes are made. We could also spend some time on our cash situation. We still have loads of cash unsafely sitting around in the U.S. The prepaid card scheme is not washing enough funds," says Ernesto. Phil pauses for one second, unsure if it is safe to be in Norrid's office in Switzerland given police scrutiny. But being with Norrid's Legal Team ahead of, and during Goang's shareholders meeting could help to counter any last-minute motion or shenanigans by KexCorp.

"Alright, we'll leave in a few hours and be there tomorrow," says Phil.

Chapter 42

A special Norrid security vehicle picks up Phil, Bianca and Tiago upon their arrival in Zurich. No sign of authorities this time around, which gives Phil a breather, especially since he hasn't yet updated Bianca on his conversations with the FBI and Interpol. Phil reminds Sergio to remain vigilant and let no one into the jet, again requiring that the pilots stay with the plane in alternating shifts.

Ernesto welcomes them in the underground garage of Norrid's head office building. He hugs the three of them one-by-one, like if they were his long-lost children, with particular attention to Bianca. Ernesto apologizes profusely to her about what happened in Macau with Li and his guys. He promises to have more security around her at all times in the future. Bianca is appreciative but tells Ernesto to keep this to reasonable levels, because she still wants some level of privacy, and extensive security details could bring undue attention.

Phil makes mental notes of the entry procedures and the office layout as they make their way through a labyrinth of doors and hallways. He wonders how the organization can fly under the radar with such security installations, which probably rival the U.S. President's bunker under the White House. Perhaps nobody outside Norrid's closed circle has ever visited. This knowledge would definitely be very valuable if Phil were ever to collaborate with the FBI.

Ernesto escorts Phil and Bianca to their guest room, a sumptuous suite with a corkscrew staircase leading to Norrid's main office floor where they will be working for a few days. Tiago will be staying next door and will be available for all emergencies. Phil can't help but assume that the office setup and on-demand security services imply that their every move will be monitored. Which, in a way, is probably better than being watched by the FBI, at least for the time being.

Ernesto suggests that they freshen up and meet for dinner in an upstairs conference room in three hours. He will invite some of the attorneys from the Legal Team, so they can start to strategize for Goang's shareholders meeting. Bianca looks at Phil with the eyes of a wounded animal, really hoping to have their first peaceful and intimate moment in days without Tiago almost sleeping in their bed. Nevertheless, Phil agrees to have a quick dinner and promises Bianca that they will be back to the room early.

Phil finds his first face-to-face meeting with Norrid's attorneys interesting but somewhat disturbing. When describing their actions and involvement with Norrid's activities, they use a legal jargon identical to the one used by the lawyers of criminals in a court of law: "our client this; we will object to that; we will file this motion, etc.". They are essentially exonerating themselves of any crime by making it sound like they are just taking various steps on behalf of their client. They must be covering their tracks well.

As he originally feared, Phil learns from the Legal Team that KexCorp has already sent multiple correspondences to Goang's counsel in an attempt to control the upcoming shareholders meeting. The procedural requests like changes of venue or attempting to dictate who will chair the meeting seem inconsequential to Phil, but he is shocked to learn that KexCorp is trying to invalidate the participation or even the votes of the mutual fund managers. While Ernesto offers to have Phil or Dr. Debo get in the middle of it, which completely frightens Phil, Norrid's Legal Team members don't seem too worried and insist on continuing to handle the issues with Goang's counsel.

Finally back to their room, Bianca's earlier desire for intimate moments with Phil seem completely abated by exhaustion and jet lag. After a few minutes of pillow talk about Bianca's planned excursion through Zurich the following day, they give in to sleep. Phil knows there is no way that he will let Bianca out of his sight but leaves the conversation for tomorrow. He needs to rest up first.

The following morning, Bianca's argument with Tiago about wanting the freedom to go sit at a nearby café, wakes Phil up. It's later than he had planned to start reviewing the tally of the proxy votes with the Legal Team.

"Bianca, why don't we send Tiago to get us some food and we can lie in bed for another half hour?" asks Phil.

"Because I refuse to give in to this life of paranoia," answers Bianca as she puts on her boots, clearly decided to head outside.

"I could really use your help today to..." Phil says but gets interrupted.

"I won't take part of your dodgy activities anymore. I just want to be a housewife," Bianca says with a smile.

"Will a jet wife suit you? Because my house is situated inside a plane," says Phil, trying to keep the conversation light.

"Yes, Mr. Jetman. I can be that girl for you," says Bianca while pushing Phil onto the bed before slowly landing on him with her arms opened, imitating a plane. Phil seizes the opportunity and grabs her tightly, then waves for Tiago to leave and get breakfast.

The back-and-forth between Norrid's Legal Team and Goang's counsel is already quite intense when Phil and Bianca join the 'party' at ten o'clock. Phil just watches as folders and documents are flying all over the busy conference room full of lawyers. He also hears Dr. Debo on the speaker phone, running down a list of shareholders that he has convinced to provide their proxy votes. They have not heard back from Equit's employees to obtain their proxies, so Phil offers to call Alex again before it's too late in Singapore.

"Hey Alex, did you get all the Goang proxies?" asks Phil.

"Yeah, we're just about to send all that stuff to you guys. But hey, the word on the street is that KexCorp stopped trying to obtain proxies a few hours ago. Some people think they've already reached the 50% they need," says Alex.

"Or they know that it's now impossible to get more. They didn't have much support from other shareholders to start with. In any case, we're still trying to block their motions," says Phil, trying to sound as confident as possible, but Alex's words are troubling. Is the battle already lost?

Around noon, all the lawyers leave the conference room and head out for lunch. Curious about the number of proxies that Norrid has accumulated thus far, Phil starts going through some of the paperwork left on the table. Lots of legal memos, letters and broker records. The name Boldwell Foundation appears at multiple places in the documents and seems to be the entity that will have the ability to vote the shares owned by Norrid as well as the proxies received so far from the efforts of Dr. Debo and Alex. Phil asks Bianca to help him go through the piles of paper to see if more information could be found about this mysterious foundation.

Bianca makes an interesting finding in one of the legal memos. The Boldwell Foundation actually owns Norrid Inc. When Ernesto first introduced Norrid to Phil, he had said that an 'unnamed individual' owned Norrid. But if a foundation owns Norrid, then essentially there is nobody at the top. A foundation is typically setup for philanthropic purposes, so no one person is benefiting from all of this criminal activity. Interesting...

Phil smiles as he thinks about the brilliance of this setup. Whichever band of criminals came up with this structure can easily escape detection by using the cover of some kind of not-for-profit organization. But who benefits? Could it be the lawyers from Norrid's Legal Team that extract all of Norrid's profits by charging mountains of legal fees? Perhaps they are not even employees of Norrid and hide their involvement in criminal activities by claiming that they are merely serving a client of their law firm.

Phil and Bianca are murmuring in the far corner of the room when Ernesto storms in and asks if they could shift gears and start working on Norrid's cash problems in the U.S. With Tiago always nearby, like a loyal dog following its master, they head to the conference room in which Bianca had worked a few weeks ago. Ernesto describes to them the increasing amounts of cash being left with street level operatives around the U.S., and potentially unsafely stored. Apparently, the prepaid card scheme has barely put a dent into the problem. The operatives not only dislike having to show their faces at various stores across the US, but they are starting to report having difficulty procuring the cards, with stores running out of them. Another scheme is immediately needed, and Phil's brilliance needs to be put to work once again.

Phil tells Ernesto that he is distracted with the Goang proxy situation and promises that he will look into the cash problem tomorrow, after Goang's shareholders meeting. But Ernesto insists that this is a pressing need, and the Legal Team is more than capable of handling the proxies. Nothing more can be accomplished on that side by Phil or Bianca. Phil agrees. He asks Ernesto to give him an update later on the count.

They sit in the conference room, knowing full well that no genius money transporting or laundering idea will come to them today. Their minds are still on the mysterious foundation that owns Norrid. There has to be a group of benefactors somewhere who are pulling Norrid's strings and benefit from the massive setup. Phil paces back and forth. From across the floor, he sees Ernesto enter the room where the legal department is working. A heated discussion seems to ensue. It sounds like bad news. Phil slowly makes his way across the floor to find out what is going on. He can hear shouting and disagreements between Ernesto and the lawyers. Suddenly, Ernesto points at them, appears to give instructions with his index finger pointing at a few of them. Then he storms out.

"Ernesto, everything ok?" asks Phil.

"It's fine, just some last minute back-and-forth with Goang," answers Ernesto.

"What is the latest count of votes and proxies under Norrid's control?" asks Phil.

"Right around 9%. I'm quite busy, I'll catch up with you later."

Assuming the mutual funds still have their 42%, and they still disagree with KexCorp, Norrid's 9% of proxies will be enough to control Goang's shareholders meeting, concludes Phil.

Chapter 43

Phil's alarm goes off at three o'clock in the morning (nine o'clock in Hong Kong) as Goang's shareholders meeting is starting. He browses the website of the South China Morning Post, which publishes live updates on the largest corporate battle of the city's recent history.

Josh is representing KexCorp in-person at the Grand Hyatt Hotel in Hong Kong, where some Goang shareholders have assembled. Minutes into the meeting, he presents a motion to replace all board members of Goang with a list of pre-qualified individuals. The motion is put to vote. After 15 minutes of movements in the room, the board's secretary passes the results to the Chairman, who announces the motion has passed with 57% of the vote. The fate of Goang is now in the hands of KexCorp.

Phil is stunned, there must be an error. He cross checks against other websites. The BBC's headline reads "a Hong Kong jewel is taken by an American conglomerate". He starts yelling obscenities and shaking his computer. Bianca wakes up, looks at the clock, and knows immediately what just happened. What a horror show.

"How is this possible?" asks Phil.

"They must have gotten some last minute proxies," says Bianca.

"The motion passed with 57%. Unless some of the mutual funds somehow got convinced to change their stance, Norrid's shares must have gotten incorrectly voted. I should have supervised the voting myself," says Phil.

They get interrupted when Phil's phone rings. He recognizes the number, it's Agent Turner. Phil takes a deep breath before answering.

"Phil, what a surprise. We really thought KexCorp would need to sweeten its offer before we could finally get involved. Now that KexCorp controls the board of Goang, the United States' Securities and Exchange Commission has purview over Goang, Equit and soon enough, we are going to ask uncomfortable questions about Norrid. Are we ready to talk cooperation?" asks Agent Turner. Phil pauses for a few seconds to contemplate his answer.

"There is a chance," answers Phil, wanting to say the least possible in front of Bianca.

"Text me your email address. I'll send you a collaboration and plea agreement," says Agent Turner.

Bianca questions Phil about who just called. He looks down and types on his phone to avoid making eye contact with her. He doesn't want to dig deeper into lies but at the same time, doesn't want to get into any details, especially in a suite inside of Norrid's office. He slowly slips back under the covers and whispers to her that they need to search for more information about the Boldwell Foundation over the next few days.

After turning and twisting in bed for another two hours, Phil decides to get up to start his search of Norrid's office before everybody else arrives. Unfortunately though, the conference room is locked, so he just roams around the empty office floor.

He decides to sit at Ernesto's executive assistant's desk and wait to confront him right when he arrives. Phil needs to know what happened with the votes during Goang's shareholders meeting. He sits back to scan the newspaper when, all of a sudden, his attention is diverted to a pink telephone message memo pad. He gets curious and looks at who called Ernesto yesterday. Interesting... Henry from KexCorp called four times. What could these two be discussing hours before Goang's shareholders meeting? Could Henry have somehow convinced Ernesto to vote Norrid's shares in favor of the KexCorp's motion? Was this the reason for Ernesto's argument with the lawyers yesterday? How could Norrid possibly benefit from any cooperation with KexCorp? How could Henry even know Ernesto well enough to call him four times within a few hours? Henry must be completely ignorant of Norrid's criminal activities. There is no way that a man of his importance would want to get anywhere close to such thugs.

An email from Agent Turner distracts Phil from his wild imagination of conspiracy theories. The plea agreement proposes a jail sentence of five to seven years for both Phil and Bianca, assuming full cooperation, including details of Norrid's activities in all countries where it operates and the names of the principal actors. Phil is sick to his stomach with the thought that Bianca would also have to serve a prison sentence.

The only trustworthy lawyer that Phil can think about – and count on – to help him with reviewing the FBI's proposal, is Antonio, his Brazilian lawyer. It's worth a try. He forwards the document to Antonio asking for his help to draft a counterproposal that would, at a minimum give full immunity to Bianca. It's still nighttime in Brazil, so Phil hopes to hear from Antonio later in the day.

Ernesto arrives at eight o'clock. He is not surprised to find Phil camped in front of his office.

"Phil, I know you are disappointed but...," says Ernesto before being interrupted by Phil.

"I hope this is a mistake, because I've seen dirty politics during my corporate life, but this would trump everything. Ernesto, how could you let this happen?" asks Phil.

"We had no choice. There is nothing I could have done. We were asked to vote all the shares that Norrid owns, and the proxies, in favor of KexCorp's motion. I do not know the reasons why," says Ernesto with a soft voice, with a hand on Phil's shoulder, trying to comfort him.

"This is a massive risk for Norrid. Did you remind people of that? And why would anyone at Norrid want to listen to pleas made by the CEO of KexCorp? It just doesn't make any sense," asks Phil, fishing for information about Henry's phone calls on the previous day. Ernesto raises his eyebrows when Phil mentions KexCorp's CEO.

"I reminded Norrid's seniors of these risks. Multiple times. And I am not sure if there was any contact between Norrid and KexCorp, or whether KexCorp's leaders put pressure on anyone at Norrid to have the proxies voted that way. Anyhow, there is apparently a plan to address the risks that you mentioned. I don't have the details yet. Look, this organization has been investigated and taken to its knees many times in the past, but we have the best lawyers in the world and we always get back up by refocusing on our roots," explains Ernesto, rehashing a line that Phil has already heard many times.

Phil doesn't want to push the conversation too much to keep his potential advantage of cooperation with the FBI. If too many people within Norrid were to realize that the authorities are about to barge into their office, others might also cooperate, reducing Phil's negotiating power. Moreover, Phil now knows that some secret relationship exists with KexCorp. Ernesto seems to deny the potential pleas made by Henry even though they called each other multiple times, hours before the crucial motion was passed by Goang's shareholders.

If Henry only knew the nature of Norrid's activities, he would have never made those calls, thinks Phil. There is no way that Henry would have taken the risk of cooperating with criminals. With the benefit of hindsight, Phil wishes that he had tipped enough information to Josh for him to feed Henry with the background of Norrid's activities.

Around mid-afternoon, Phil receives an e-mail from Antonio. He says he would be happy to help but reminds Phil that he will eventually have to hire a lawyer, who is a member of the Bar of whichever state he would get prosecuted from. Presumably the State of New York, Antonio suggests. In any case, Antonio's first advice is to counter-propose with a request for full exoneration and immunity for both Phil and Bianca, for all past crimes in all countries covered by both the FBI and Interpol. Phil smiles when he reads Antonio's e-mail, he likes his aggressiveness. He also likes the idea that his years of white-collar crime while working for KexCorp would be completely behind him. A peaceful and safe life in the U.S. – or in any developed country – with Bianca would be possible again.

While Bianca is busy looking through the piles of documents for any clues regarding the Boldwell Foundation, Phil steps out, asks Tiago to stay with Bianca, and goes down to the street to get a coffee. With no one to eavesdrop on him, Phil calls Agent Turner.

"Phil, good to hear from you in such short time. I thought I would have to follow up with you today, so I'm glad you called, which tells me that you've come to the realization that we've cornered you," says Agent Turner, with a wide smile, so proud of what he thinks is sophisticated police work.

"Always a pleasure. Look, I'm not sure if this is going to work," bluffs Phil, then pauses.

"Really? I actually thought that you had come to your senses for a moment," says Agent Turner.

"Well, you know, like I said before I'm really worried about breaching the non-disclosure agreements with my clients, and your whole jail time really doesn't make sense for innocent people," says Phil.

"Phil, it's just a question of time before...," says Agent Turner but Phil interrupts.

"We both know you don't have anything. And the Securities and Exchange Commission would take months to even be able to start an investigation, and who knows where that would lead. Listen, if I'm going to sign anything with you, it has to give Bianca and I complete immunity from the jurisdictions of the FBI and Interpol, for any possible crime whatsoever up to the time of signing the agreement. That way, I'll be protected from my clients' prosecutions, and from any law enforcement agency that would want to drag me into the activities of my clients. And my cooperation would allow you to move so much quicker. It's a real win-win situation," requests Phil.

"You're completely dreaming. You would need to provide criminal information leading to the arrest of a well-known public figure to strike this kind of deal," says Agent Turner.

Phil pauses for a second. Thinking about yesterday's calls from Henry to Ernesto. There may be enough pulling of strings by Henry to qualify for the kind of celebrity criminal that Agent Turner is talking about. Or at a minimum, dragging Henry into the fray might earn Phil enough credits with the FBI to get him out of significant trouble.

"Well Agent Turner, you might actually get what you wish for. I'll send you a marked-up copy of the collaboration agreement. Let me know what you think," says Phil, hoping that the FBI doesn't completely back out of the deal at a later stage if they find out that Henry's calls to Ernesto were not incriminating. There is a strong possibility, after all, that Henry doesn't even know that Norrid is a criminal organization.

Chapter 44

Although still closely monitored by Tiago, Phil decides that it is now the time to initiate their escape. They hop on the jet and Phil announces that they are heading to Bali. But a few minutes before takeoff, he sneaks into the cockpit and tells Sergio that the destination is Nassau, Bahamas, and asks him to keep it a secret from Bianca and Tiago.

Eight hours later, minutes before landing, Phil lets out the surprise that they are arriving in the Bahamas, not Bali. Bianca swiftly looks through the window and marvels at the turquoise water surrounding the islands. She looks like a child on Christmas Day. Tiago, however, looks at Phil suspiciously and is unhappy to have gone in the opposite direction of where he was expecting. Navy Seals like to have everything planned out, so Tiago is visibly uncomfortable with a location that he hasn't studied in advance. As he reaches for his phone, Phil puts a hand on Tiago's shoulder.

"Tiago, please trust me with this, it's better if we remain under the radar for the time being. I'll explain everything soon," says Phil, hoping that Tiago doesn't alert anyone at Norrid.

"This better be good," replies Tiago, sternly looking into Phil's eyes. Bianca feels nervous but watches in silence as the two men seem to bond for the first time.

Although the plane is still taxiing, Claudio comes out of the cockpit and announces that they were ordered to taxi to a special immigration and customs location. Phil and Tiago scramble to hide money, weapons and computers in the safe, which they then place in the usual hiding spot: under the mattress.

Upon disembarking, they are met by Agent Turner and Agent Dia. They introduce themselves as working for the FBI and Interpol respectively. Bianca remembers meeting Agent Dia a few months ago but pretends, as Phil does, to meet them for the first time, so that Tiago would not get any wrong impression. The agents ask that everyone leave their luggage on the plane and all personal effects in boxes at the entrance of the terminal. They then go through metal detectors, which reveal that Tiago had kept a cell phone strapped to his ankle. Agent Turner grabs the phone and gives a dirty look to Tiago. Each of them, including the pilots, is placed in a separate interrogation room. The two agents enter Phil's room.

"We're glad that you asked us to meet you here," says Agent Turner.

"Yeah, well, I didn't quite expect that you'd meet us on arrival. Hopefully you've taken all precautions to avoid that Tiago or any other Norrid operative become aware that I'm talking to you," says Phil.

"Don't worry. I actually think that we have a chance to make Tiago collaborate as well," says Agent Dia.

"So, we reviewed your counter-proposal for full immunity for Bianca and yourself. We have approval from our superiors, as long as you agree to help us tap the celebrity criminal that is involved with Norrid," says Agent Turner.

"Tap? As in recording of a random conversation?" asks Phil, trying to escape with an easy task.

"No. Tap, as in recording a person confessing to a criminal act," says Agent Dia. Phil tighten his lips, expressing the potential difficulty in doing that.

"Well, I would have thought that this type of thing would be part of your job description, not mine. I can agree to try on a best efforts basis. The person is quite smart, so I would say the outcome would depend on various factors," says Phil.

"Arresting that person will be an absolute condition. Your freedom is not assured until the arrest. Who are we talking about?" asks Agent Turner.

"First, show me our cooperation agreement, with signatures from the superiors of both of your organizations. I won't reveal my most valuable piece of information unless you guys can come through with what you promised," says Phil.

They show the document to Phil, which he takes several minutes to study. Full impunity and immunity, for both Phil and Bianca, from prosecutions for any crime whatsoever is well documented and explained in the document. Phil can barely believe his eyes. He is surprised that they would even offer this to him. They must be so desperate for a break in this case.

"Okay. So, I suggest that we bring Bianca in here, I'll explain everything to her, and if she agrees, we sign this and simultaneously tell you the name of the person," suggests Phil.

"Fine with us, but if you don't give us the name or refuse to sign, we arrest you both," says Agent Turner in an aggressive tone, trying to impose his way.

"Could you please stop your bluff? It's so obvious that you have no evidence against us. We're collaborating here, so be nice," says Phil.

Agent Turner leaves the room and comes back five minutes later with Bianca. She is somewhat on the edge, so Phil calms her down and explains the whole situation to her, focusing primarily on the immunity that they would receive with this collaboration agreement.

"That all sounds great but won't Norrid operatives pursue us for the rest of our lives?" asks Bianca, worried that police cooperation might actually be a death sentence.

"They will all be in jail," says Agent Dia categorically.

"Some will, others won't. We need protection. We need to cut Tiago into this deal and keep him with us for the foreseeable future. He is the only one that we can trust. He is not the guy you're looking for anyway, he is basically just a sophisticated security guard," says Bianca. Phil nods in agreement. The two agents look at each other and see no problem. It may actually be less responsibilities and headaches if they do not have to worry about having to dispatch officers to protect Phil and Bianca with some kind of witness protection program.

"This shouldn't be a problem. We'll get another agreement drafted for him. Can we get this one signed now?" asks Agent Turner.

"Alright," says Phil as he starts signing the documents along with Bianca. "And the person that is at least tangentially involved with Norrid, and that you need to investigate is Henry Dylerman, CEO of KexCorp Industries."

Agents Turner and Dia sport a wide smile, partially from their astonishment, but primarily because they are licking their chops, like kids in a candy store, at the thought of having their names associated with catching a well-known celebrity CEO. Especially someone of Henry's stature, who supposedly is a high-profile advocate of ethical behavior in New York City. That would be such an irony. The Agents immediately feel like they could actually make their career with this case, and even perhaps get a lucrative book or movie deal, just for being the ones making such an arrest.

Although Phil's stomach is tense from snitching on the man that provided a long and successful career to him, he feels like he had given enough warnings about connecting KexCorp to Goang, especially through Josh, but also Ernesto. Assuming Henry received the warnings through either or both of them, he has brought this one onto himself.

Phil can sense the excitement and vibe of the Agents in front of him. Therefore, he takes the opportunity to insist that Tiago is brought into the deal right away.

Chapter 45

The FBI and Interpol each send two additional agents to Nassau in order to download every bit of information from Phil, Bianca and Tiago. Packed in a small office in Nassau, Phil spends countless hours explaining Norrid's schemes to the authorities. The agents cannot believe the sophistication, especially with the work of the Raptors and Chameleons operating the currency booths and the crypto scheme that have brought in so much money into Equit. It makes Phil wonder if any law enforcement agency would have ever been able to catch him without cooperation. In any case, getting immunity for his past crimes is much more valuable than his meager 'salary' with Norrid, particularly if Phil is able to salvage his fortune hidden in bank accounts all over the world, given that authorities will not go after him for his past crimes.

However, Phil has no illusions. He knows that he traded one threat for another. Having the authorities on his side only means that it's a question of time before Norrid learns that he, Bianca and Tiago have become snitches. Therefore, Phil continually insists on the guilt of life-threatening criminals like Li, who really needs to be taken off the streets along with his thugs. On the other hand, Phil attempts to deemphasize the role of Dr. Debo. For no rational reason, Phil believes that Dr. Debo deserves to escape prosecution.

While Bianca and Tiago participate in some of the meetings, most of the time they are free. Phil instructs them to work with Paul and Linda to have the yacht ready to go at any moment. They hoard onto the boat cash in numerous currency denominations, satellite phones, security equipment and food supplies that would potentially last them weeks, maybe months, while navigating around the Caribbean Sea, or beyond. Perhaps even down to Brazil.

The yacht, with its four bedrooms, provides plenty of privacy, which had been missing in Phil and Bianca's life lately, with Tiago sleeping steps away from them. Plus, Bianca is rejuvenated by daily drinking sessions with Linda, the immunity agreements, and the prospects of a life with Phil, alternating between the jet and the yacht. She keeps Phil awake for multiple nights in row with more intimacy than Phil had ever imagined or hoped for. He is very happy to take his mind away from the stressful situation with the Agents. In particular, he dreads the moment when he will need to deliver on his last contractual obligation with the FBI: recording Henry while making him admit his interaction with Norrid to seal off the takeover of Goang.

That moment comes soon enough. Agent Turner announces that Phil will have to call Henry and propose to come in as a consultant to help KexCorp with the integration of Goang, just like he has done on numerous occasions throughout his career. And then, Phil needs to suggest a meeting in New York to make Henry talk about how he successfully steered through the offer for Goang, the proxy fight and the shareholders meeting. The objective is to make him say something about Norrid. Just enough to allow questioning, search, and eventually, an arrest warrant.

Phil doesn't like the idea of meeting Henry at KexCorp's offices in New York. Henry is a powerful manipulator and if Ernesto already shared too much information with him, he could easily turn the tables on Phil for his involvement with Norrid. Or even worse, what if Henry has figured out by now that Phil has stolen hundreds of millions from KexCorp? And this is all going be recorded by the FBI. For the moment, however, Phil doesn't have a choice. He needs to fulfill this one last condition of his cooperation and immunity contract with the law enforcement agencies.

The call with Henry turns out to be a piece of cake. After a few pleasantries and congratulations by Phil to Henry for having pulled off the replacement of Goang's board, Henry turns nostalgic on Phil and pleads with him to come back to work for KexCorp. Phil says that he is enjoying retirement too much for a full-time job but would not mind helping out for a few months. They agree to meet in New York the following day.

The night before heading out, Phil assembles his whole crew on the yacht for a dinner: Bianca, Paul, Linda, Tiago, Sergio and Claudio. Reminiscent of the emotional moments of the Fast & Furious movies, Phil refers to them as 'family'.

"Sergio and Claudio will take me to New York tomorrow. I have an important meeting that only I can attend, before we can get to the next chapter of our lives," declares Phil solemnly.

"Who is going to protect you? I should go with you," says Tiago.

"No, I would rather that you stay on the yacht and protect Bianca, Paul and Linda. And I have a request that is very important for the safety of all of us: as soon as I step off this boat, you need to sail off to the open sea, and remain at large, untraceable, even by myself, until I contact you again on the satellite phones. My mission may take hours, days, weeks, I don't know. But when I do contact you, I will say the word 'freedom' followed by the initials of the Caribbean airport where I want you to pick me up. After that, Sergio and Claudio will fly the jet off to Brazil and keep it there until it is safe for us to fly again," explains Phil, wanting to give them an escape in case he is unable to generate Henry's confession, which would void the immunity agreements. Phil then turns toward Sergio with a smile. "You guys will have a well-deserved vacation back home for a few months. Don't get too comfortable though, we're going to call on you again soon."

"Anytime sir," says Sergio, like a soldier.

"Phil, your trip to New York sounds very serious, will you update us on this important mission? Can we help?" asks Paul.

"No offense Paul, but for Tiago's safety, we're going to limit your duties to be captain of this boat," says Phil with a smile, referring to their late-night adventure in Kuala Lumpur. Everyone smiles and Paul puts his arm around Tiago's shoulder as a form of apology.

"Well, we are glad to share these memories with you all, and look forward to continue this journey together soon," says Linda, while raising her wine glass to cheer everyone.

Phil's plane lands in Teterboro, New Jersey, minutes from New York City, at noon on the following day. The plane was gutted from anything illegal, so no stress, this time around, to clear immigration and customs. A black limousine is waiting for Phil on the tarmac. He is not surprised that the car is packed with four FBI agents ready to equip him with sophisticated recording and filming devices. They also give Phil the latest instructions about his encounter with Henry.

By the time Phil is let into Henry's office, it is past four o'clock. Henry is in a good mood. He has a victory look on his face, emboldened by KexCorp's battle for Goang.

"Good to see you Phil. Thank you for coming to help us with this acquisition," says Henry.

"It's my pleasure. I don't know Goang too well though. I just followed parts of the back-and-forth of the proxy fight in the newspapers. What is it like to deal with them?" asks Phil, trying to dance around the main issues.

"You'll get to know them soon enough. Why don't you hop on a plane and meet Josh in Hong Kong tomorrow to finalize the due diligence agreement with the board?" says Henry, not really asking but more dictating in his usual military commander ways, moving his troops wherever needed. Phil becomes nervous about Henry's expectations to go to Hong Kong. Making Henry admit things imply spending time with him in New York, not 10,000 miles away.

"Actually, I was hoping to work from New York for at least of few days. I haven't been back here since I resigned, so I have a few personal things to handle," lies Phil.

"No problem, you can spend the next couple of days here and then take a flight to Hong Kong during the weekend. You'll be ready to work with Goang's team Monday morning. Listen, I have to run but head over to Human Resources, they'll onboard you on a contract for three months. I've already told them to pay you $8,000 per week, I hope that's ok with you," says Henry.

"That's very generous, thank you. Say, are you free for dinner tonight?" asks Phil.

"Busy tonight. But I can do tomorrow," says Henry.

"Sounds like a plan, thank you. We'll be able to cover..." says Phil, but cannot finish his sentence, Henry is already heading to a conference room for a meeting.

Making Henry sit down and talk freely about his interactions with Norrid is not going to be easy. Phil heads back to his jet and huddles with Agents Turner and Dia to brainstorm about ways to make Henry open up. What if Phil brought up shocking news about Goang? Perhaps he could raise the prospects of Equit's employees wanting a management buyout. Or even worse, reveal to Henry that Equit is a money laundering operation for Norrid. Maybe this could be enough to get him started on revelations.

Chapter 46

Henry and Phil meet at the Harvard Club of New York City, a social club exclusive to graduates of Harvard University. They sit in a corner of the dining room, sufficiently far away from any other guest, so that their conversation would not be heard.

In line with his usual statesman behavior, Henry directs the waiters to attend his refined tastes and needs, as if he owned the place. Although Phil is not impressed, he makes believe that he has never seen such a beautiful and exclusive club, and pretends to appreciate Henry's seemingly Governor-like status.

After a few minutes of meaningless pleasantries, Phil decides to jump right into his mission.

"So, Henry, I've been doing some research about Goang and their joint venture Equit. Did you know that the management team is very displeased with the prospects of potentially being part of KexCorp, and want a management buyout?" asks Phil.

"Of course I'm aware, it was in the papers a few weeks ago. We're going to solve this soon by buying the partner out and giving no voice to Equit's management team. This is going to be a KexCorp company, full stop," says Henry.

"Apparently they are very good at what they do. Don't you think they'd be dissatisfied and leave?" asks Phil.

"Perhaps. But they are under contracts, at least in the short term. We can offer them some incentives to sign them up for longer. It's all about the money, you know that Phil, don't you?" says Henry.

"Right... look, the other thing that I want to make sure you're aware of is that there are rumors that Equit is being used to launder money for the other partner. If I were to start doing the due diligence for you, I wouldn't want to be associated with this kind of practice. The name of the organization is Norrid. Have you heard of them before?" asks Phil, starting to lay the trap that he had agreed with the FBI.

"You're bothered by the activities of Norrid? It didn't bother you that much before," says Henry. Phil raises his eyebrows, puzzled by Henry's words. Phil pauses for a few seconds, looking into Henry's eyes.

"What do you mean?" asks Phil, afraid of Henry's potential creepy knowledge of his involvement with Norrid.

"You know exactly what I mean. Did you really think I had no idea what you were up to since you 'retired' from KexCorp? A man of my importance cannot let someone like you retire in his early 40s. You are in the prime of your career. It was suspicious to say the least. Anyway, it all turned out for the best. The innovations that you brought in over the past year are worth billions for KexCorp," explains Henry, proud of the turn of events.

"Worth billions for KexCorp? Are you trying some reverse psychology on me? You may have committed KexCorp to its death sentence by associating it with Norrid. How on earth do you see value for KexCorp in a money laundering scheme? Am I the only one on this planet aware of the severity of money laundering crimes?" blurts Phil, as he goes off the script that he agreed with the Agents and gets carried away by his frustration during months of efforts trying to avoid a takeover of Goang. He cannot help but ask these questions directly to Henry. Perhaps he would continue with his pride and explanations. And finally reveal his connection with Norrid.

"Relax Phil. I know you're smart, but you haven't fully thought through the potential that Norrid offers to KexCorp. The money inflows from Norrid's currency booths and into Equit will continue for the foreseeable future. You've actually setup the scheme that I needed to keep Goang and all of KexCorp's Asian operations afloat," says Henry.

"The scheme that YOU needed?" asks Phil, raising his voice slightly to make sure that the FBI agents are closely listening.

"Exactly, I needed it. Norrid already has other schemes to inject funds into dozens of KexCorp's companies. Cash flows from Norrid's activities are making KexCorp more powerful than ever. I have setup the Boldwell foundation for this very reason: take money from questionable sources, wash it through the pipes of Norrid, buy goods and services from KexCorp, and make me a 'hero CEO' for never missing any earnings target. The model is simple, we just temporarily push money exactly where it needs to go to patch up any struggling operation owned by KexCorp," explains Henry.

"Brilliant," says Phil, feeling sweat dampen the back of his shirt. Henry perceives Phil's smile as an approval, but in reality, Phil is enjoying his personal victory. He just discovered that Henry was hiding in plain sight. A successful CEO that always says the right thing. A philanthropist that even sets up a foundation to complete the perfect structure. That is, until it gets discovered by officially connecting KexCorp and Norrid through the

Equit joint venture. Phil has now delivered much more than the authorities had expected. And they are listening to all this. It's all music to Phil's ears. He just earned his freedom.

"I am so glad to have you back with KexCorp. And don't worry, there is no risk for you. KexCorp only touches money that is already laundered. Except, of course, for Li's complete idiocy to deposit cash into Equit's account. This guy really needs to be dealt with," says Henry, now openly assuming his role of organized crime leader.

"Yeah, tell me about it. But, if you were tracking me all along, and you're behind all of Norrid's activities, why did you even agree that Norrid enters into the joint venture with Goang? Wasn't that taking some opportunities away from Norrid, by sharing with Goang?" asks Phil.

"That's what I also thought at first. But then, I realized that by buying Goang, I could legitimize KexCorp's investment in Equit without completely, directly and officially partnering with Norrid. Everything turned out for the best. Stupid Li, however, almost messed up everything with his insider trading of Goang stock, I hadn't seen that one coming," says Henry.

"Me neither," says Phil, in complete disbelief that Henry is not realizing the magnitude of his mistakes.

Phil continues to listen but realizes that despite his masterful setup of Boldwell and Norrid, and the steady injection of laundered money into KexCorp, Henry had become overly confident and hadn't fully assessed the risks associated with his takeover of Goang. His ego probably had a lot to do with his determination to keep pressing for the acquisition, despite all the red flags that came along the way. This move was clearly one step too far in his quest to dominate the world by simultaneously running one of the biggest companies in the world, and the most sophisticated criminal organization.

Phil is now eager to get out of there, before Henry figures out that he is being recorded. At this point, going into hiding in the Caribbeans is an absolute must until the dust settles. Henry's involvement with Norrid is frightening and his potential arrest will make headlines all over the world. Also, Henry must have so many resources to track down people, so escaping is the only way. Phil is also getting nervous that the 'trigger happy' FBI agents would barge into the Harvard Club for an immediate arrest of Henry. Phil needs to leave at the first opportunity.

The dinner drags to eleven o'clock. Phil is genuinely exhausted, excuses himself for the night, and to continue his ruse, promises to Henry that he will see him in the morning. He hops onto a yellow taxi to take him back to the Teterboro airport.

Phil's adrenaline is still high, however. He feels that, at any moment, Henry would realize that he had been trapped and would send thugs chasing after him.

Agents Turner and Dia are waiting for Phil in the hanger where his jet is parked. They are absolutely ecstatic about the details that Phil was able to obtain. The agents are armed with two bottles of Veuve Clicquot champagne, ready to celebrate, while a warrant is being obtained in Manhattan for Henry's arrest.

But Phil turns them down on the celebration, wanting to be in the air as soon as possible. He insists however, to immediately have a document indicating that he fulfilled the condition of his collaboration and immunity agreement. The Agents offer to send it to him on the following day, but Phil wants to leave with something, so they just hand write a few sentences on a memo pad, which Phil will safely keep forever.

Phil tells Sergio to file a flight plan to Nassau and depart immediately but to expect a destination change as soon as they exit the U.S. airspace. He wonders if he is being too paranoid, but at this point, nothing would surprise him.

Then, he texts Bianca:

Freedom G.T.

Made in the USA
Middletown, DE
09 November 2022

14347495R00166